Planning An
Early Childhood Program

Written and Illustrated by
Marie Keenan

PEGUIS PUBLISHERS
WINNIPEG • CANADA

Canadian Cataloguing in Publication Data

Keenan, Marie, 1942–

Children first

Originally published: Calgary : Braun and Braun Educational Enterprises, 1988.
Includes bibliographical references.
ISBN 1-895411-51-3

1. Education, Preschool. I. Title.

LB1140.2.K44   1993   372.21   C93-098074-3

Peguis Publishers Ltd.
520 Hargrave Street
Winnipeg, MB
Canada R3A 0X8

Cover Design: Laura Ayers

Printed and bound in Canada

69013

Contents

iii

Appendices

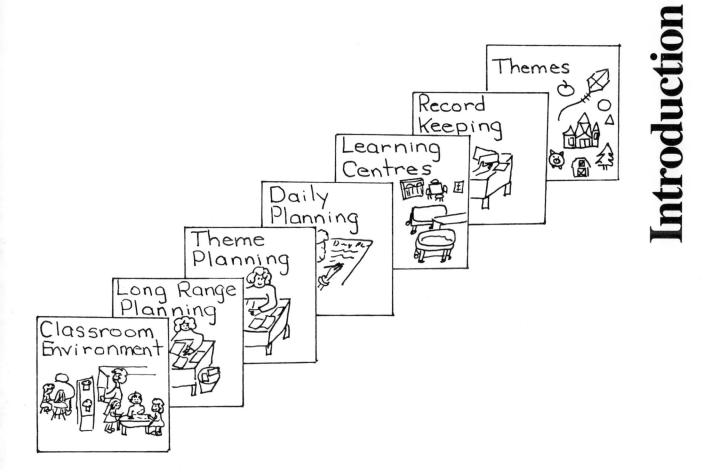

Teachers of early childhood programs have developed many ways of planning and organizing for optimum learning. My experiences as a teacher of young children, and as an early childhood consultant, have provided opportunities for me to experiment extensively with many forms of planning and organization. In this book I want to share with teachers some of the ways of planning and implementing programs which I have found to be most successful. It is my hope that beginning as well as experienced teachers will find the suggestions useful in working with young children.

I have identified six main steps to consider when planning an early childhood program. These steps are consistent with the six chapters of this book. Each step should be regarded as equally important in effective program planning. Following is a brief outline of each of these steps:

• Step one is the consideration I give to atmosphere and physical space in the classroom and this is discussed in Chapter One. The ideas presented in this chapter have been influenced by actual comments from children, as well as through my personal experiences.

• Step two is the way in which I use long range planning to establish the basic organization of the program which is discussed in Chapter Two. This chapter also discusses the necessary ingredients for long range planning, describes long range plans, gives examples of plans, and provides a sequencing format.

• Using themes as overall topics in program planning is step three. One method of using themes as an approach to planning is provided in Chapter Three. A sample theme is used to demonstrate in a step by step way, how I use a thematic format in theme planning.

• Step four is daily planning which is described in Chapter Four. The importance I give to well-organized, well-written daily plans is emphasized in this chapter. A blank daily plan format as well as a completed format based on the theme plan introduced in Chapter Three is provided.

• The fifth step described in Chapter Five considers important points that I like to keep in mind when planning centres. This chapter also discusses the range in children's abilities which must be provided for through activities at any learning centre. The role of the teacher and guidelines for establishing routines are covered in Chapter Five as well.

• My sixth step is record keeping which is described in Chapter Six. I have found that keeping thorough records is a very important step in effective program planning. This chapter provides a combination of reasons for record keeping and practical ideas for implementing good record keeping.

The appendix of this book provides a variety of theme plans that I have developed and used. These theme plans show how curriculum ideas and learning opportunities in a given topic area are integrated into every part of an early childhood program.

This book is dedicated to the children

who have taught me so much about teaching.

1

Introduction

First impressions are powerful when people experience particular thoughts and feelings as they encounter a new environment or meet new people. In my visits to many classrooms I have become aware of how people can be affected by initial impressions of the atmosphere and physical arrangement of the classroom.

The classroom atmosphere grows from the teacher's philosophy of teaching. How the environment is structured reflects the teacher's ideas about how children develop. The following sections discuss the importance of considering atmosphere and physical arrangement in planning a program for young children.

Atmosphere

The increasingly complex society in which we live is the source of much tension. This tension is registered in the feelings and actions of young children. As I interact with young children I experience the varied extent to which they are affected by the rapid pace and anxious states which many adults experience in their personal lives. I have also seen how conscious attention to the atmosphere of everyday classroom living can create an effective buffer for these tensions.

Promoting an atmosphere which is warm, relaxed, and quiet provides opportunities for children to develop skills both in and out of the classroom that will help to reduce stress and maintain an underlying serenity. Children notice and are affected by their environment more than we think. This is most evident when they talk about how they see things. Their reactions give us vital clues about their perception of the way we communicate with them. The following section shows how children see things in their classroom world.

How Children See Things

Children have their own way of saying what it is that makes them feel good. I conducted individual interviews with twenty children from five different classrooms. These children ranged in age from five to eight years. Each child was asked, "What is it about your classroom that makes you feel good?" The children's responses were then categorized into the kinds of things the children felt made them feel good in a classroom.

The representative responses which follow clearly express categories of things and ideas for creating an atmosphere that would "feel good" to a young child.

Children notice people

Children are observant. They are likely more effective monitors of feelings than adults. Such a generalization certainly seems to come from these words from children:

Children notice displays

Positive self images are built as they see tangible attempts to communicate through different media displayed (e.g., art, writing, etc.), or personal things (e.g., birthdays) recognized on bulletin boards. Expressions of pride about self come through in the following words of young children:

You can even get to take staples out and other things for the teacher. I like that sort of because you sort of get to be responsible, and that is good.
(8 years)

I feel good when I see the things we make hanging up on the walls.
(6 years)

The teacher. She is nice and when she is angry she snaps out of it real fast and then she is happy again.
(6 years)

When I look at the birthday Care Bears on that wall, they make me feel good.
(5 years)

The teachers, because they are really nice, and they co-operate with all the kids.
(8 years)

You [the teacher] make me feel good because you smile at me when I smile at you, and you are very nice.
(5 years)

When your things are on the wall it makes you feel good, like when we did that stuff about space — that was good.
(8 years)

4

Children notice the decorating of the room

The initial appearance of a classroom can create a feeling of harmony and acceptance within children. An easier transition between home and school is made when children see school as a nice place to be.

> I like the blue things because I don't have a really favourite colour and it makes me feel like I like blue. Also if everything was the same colour, like bright, then I would feel sad. I know I would.
> (7 years)

> I like the plants in the room. My mom has plants like those kind too.
> (5 years)

> The colours are different. Some colours are bright and some colours are dull and that looks better than if all the colours were bright or all the colours were dull.
> (7 years)

> Everything has colours and that makes me feel good.
> (6 years)

Children notice materials

The following quotes from children indicate that materials which are displayed in attractive ways motivate children's interest in them, and help to make the transition from home to school:

> The calendar makes me feel good because my mom is going to have a baby, and it makes me know that every day is a new day.
> (7 years)

> The books standing up like that make me feel like I'd like to look at them.
> (5 years)

Children notice classroom arrangement

A carefully prepared physical environment leads to children's interest in one another. Through talk children learn to use language meaningfully, develop interpersonal skills, and increase their social competence. Children readily notice how the room arrangement will facilitate their own need to interact.

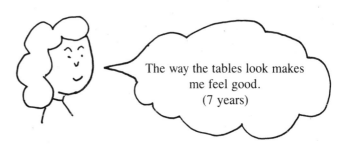

> The way the tables look makes me feel good.
> (7 years)

The above quotations emphasize the importance of providing opportunities for children to express how they are affected in a positive way by their environment. The quotations also remind teachers that children have their own ways of describing how they are affected by different things in the classroom. We are reminded as well that interviewing children is a very worthwhile activity, and one in which we can more easily identify both general and more specific needs of children.

The following section elaborates on how children may be affected by the way we communicate with them.

Communicating With Children

Communication is intertwined throughout the child's life through both verbal and body language. The way we communicate may reflect our feelings of the moment, and young children are more adept at making interpretations than we often realize. The stage of children's language development and their limited background of experiences in making sense of the talk of others strongly affects their interpretations. In a recent discussion, children were asked "What makes you sad?" Many children talked about instances in their lives that caused feelings of sadness. The following responses give us examples of how our communications may affect young children:

When people get mad at me I feel really sad, and they don't say why they are mad, then I just keep feeling sad. They keep mad at me and don't tell me why, and I get scared to ask why. I just feel sad.
(8 years)

My mom said if I practiced my violin and fixed my bed then she would give me a present, but she never.
(5 years)

Like when we move lots of times then I feel sad about my friends, and my mom says it's okay, I'll get new ones, but I still feel sad about my friends, specially Shawn.
(7 years)

These contributions leave the impression that as well as feeling 'sad' some children may also be learning to mistrust adults. Stories of promises that were not kept, adults saying things are easy when they really were not for the child, and unclear or mixed messages provide examples of adult talk that can be very confusing to a child. As teachers we can build trust and confidence, and affect a child's self concept by the way we communicate verbally and nonverbally.

My role as a teacher is to work 'with' the children, to guide and supervise, but even more importantly, it is to build a trusting climate that is caring, open, and honest. It is useful to get children to express themselves openly in private conferences to find what they like and do not like about school. This also helps children understand that you have feelings just as they do, and that you care about them just as they care about you. This gives them the feeling that they have a contribution to make toward their own environment and develop responsible attitudes. By the same token, children need to know what you like and do not like. Such an exchange provides a basis for community. Children like to be with an adult who is happy, cheerful, and content.

As adults we have a great influence on each child's developing self concept. See Figure 1-1 for the guidelines I find help children feel good about themselves when we communicate with them.

My Suggestions For Teachers

1. Smile and be cheerful. When a teacher is truly effective in communicating satisfaction and joy in teaching, this is transmitted to others in the classroom.
2. When a child wants to talk, let him know you are interested by stopping what you are doing and listening with interest.
3. When talking with a child, avoid towering over him. It is much better to sit or stoop and elicit eye to eye contact.
4. Maintain the idea that the child is operating independently; even if asked, do not lift or carry the child. Hug or comfort the child with his feet on the ground.
5. Use a quiet, well modulated voice at all times. A loud intimidating voice may startle or frighten a young child.
6. Be consistent with rules and in what you say you will or will not do. Use a quiet, but firm voice when reminding about rules. Try not to make children feel guilty or bad by intimidating them with a loud or accusing voice.
7. Discuss topics intelligently with the child and avoid talking 'down' to or 'at' a child. Children are proud of their knowledge and by acknowledging what they know, we help to build or maintain their positive self concept.
8. Demonstrate interest by accepting and acknowledging a child's feelings. Let 'him' tell you how he feels, rather than you telling him. Through talking about his own feelings, a child also develops a better understanding of himself.
9. Use nonverbal cues to show children that you are interested in what is being said. Children notice facial cues especially, so it is important to smile and look directly into their faces when interacting with them.

Figure 1-1

By being aware of how children are affected by the atmosphere of the classroom we will be more considerate in the way we communicate with them. We can also be more aware of how to respond to inappropriate behaviour and realize the importance of establishing routines. Next, I will discuss how I deal with inappropriate behaviour and how I establish routines.

Responding to Inappropriate Behaviour

As children grow and develop, their sense of autonomy also develops. By the time children reach the early years in school, they have learned to avoid doing things that create self doubt, particularly things they cannot do well.

I have found that reducing stress in the classroom also helps to reduce inappropriate behaviour. Quiet voices, subdued colours, lighting that is not too bright or glaring are all helpful ways of reducing stress for both the child and the teacher.

It is not possible to discuss each type of inappropriate behaviour, however when inappropriate behaviour must be dealt with, I deal with it as soon as possible. The list on Figure 1-2 represents a mere sampling of possible solutions.

My Suggestions For Teachers

1. If a child persists in arguing, put a stop to it by saying something like, "We've both said what we think, and still do not agree, so let's get on to something else."

2. Time out, if used sparingly and with firmness, is very useful. The time out must be where the child is visible to the teacher at all times. Time out is particularly useful if the child is aware of what is going on between the teacher and the other children, yet cannot be a part of it.

3. Channel the child's interest away from undesirable behaviour. A sudden change of topic, routine, or position (standing or sitting) can often divert interest.

4. State positively what should happen, rather than focusing on what should not happen. (e.g, Rather than, "Johnny, don't stand on the book." say, "Johnny, please pick up the book and place it on the table.")

5. Logical consequences are often effective (e.g., if a child seems to deliberately make others wait for him to join the group, begin without him).

Figure 1-2

Establishing Routines

I have found that establishing consistent routines is important in developing a tension reduced and relaxed atmosphere. Young children exhibit feelings of security when they know what is expected of them and what they may expect. Children are flexible but will more easily go along with the changes if they understand them in terms of what usually happens throughout the day.

The tone for a cooperative atmosphere can be set by expressing the need for cooperation and by reinforcing an understanding of behaviour in terms of helping one another. I have found that children operate best in a relaxed, unhurried environment in which they know the routines, guidelines, and expectations. See Figure 1-3 for the ideas I find helpful when establishing routines in the classroom.

My Suggestions For Teachers

1. Talk about the day's activities with the children early in the day to help them remember and understand the regular and new classroom routines and expectations.

2. When children are authorized to be 'helpers' or to do a task, stipulate specific duties.

3. Introduce each activity to the total group and then reinforce rules and expectations to smaller groups of individuals.

4. Develop responsible behaviour by involving the children in the development of rules and encourage expressions of reasons for rules.

5. Establish specific routines and rules for cooperation at cleanup.

6. Encourage helping behaviour which facilitates the work or play activities of others (e.g., sharing, giving information, assisting others).

7. Post ideas for volunteers in the classroom that will help in reinforcing rules and establishing routines.

Figure 1-3

The arrangement of the physical space in the classroom also has an effect on both children and adults who spend time there.

Physical Space

Children, staff, and volunteers (parents and others) all have particular needs to be considered when planning space. The following sections discuss some of their major needs and how they may be met.

Children

Each child needs an environment in which the physical arrangement is conducive to his interaction with others, where he can be alone if he wants to, and where he can move easily from one area to another. Space must be arranged so the child has ample opportunity to develop an interest and a curiosity in different materials and displays, where he is able to express himself in a whole group, small group, or on an individual basis.

Consideration must also be given to possible noise levels from different centres, to sensitivity to noise, and to providing display areas at the children's eye level.

Staff (teachers, teacher-aides)

The room arrangement must take into account the teacher's need for ease of supervision and easy access to all areas of the room. Space must be available for preparation of materials, for planning, and for storing personal articles. The physical arrangement must also take into account the fact that loud noise can be stressful to adults as well as children.

Volunteers (parents, students)

The physical arrangement has an impact on the degree of comfort felt by volunteers. Volunteers should have easy access to all areas of the room if their assistance is to be most effective. They should have a special area for preparing materials, an area for storage of personal articles, and if possible, an area for coffee, tea, and relaxation.

Most early childhood textbooks which discuss physical space also provide helpful floor plan ideas for arranging classrooms, and these should be consulted. The following sections on arranging the room, organizing, displaying, and setting out equipment and materials provide practical guidelines to assist in room arrangement.

Arranging the Classroom

The classroom arrangement must recognize that children are alike as well as different in many ways and must encourage child-child, child-materials, and child-adult interaction. Experience has taught me that the arrangement of space in the classroom must be fluid and flexible to constant change. I find the considerations listed in Figure 1-4 useful when arranging the classroom.

My Suggestions For Teachers

1. Consider fixed display areas, light sources, water sources, and storage before arranging the room.

2. Provide an open space which takes advantage of natural or artificial light sources for large group meetings where sharing, story time, discussions, and group writing projects may take place.

3. Noise barriers, ways of absorbing sound and/or distance should separate active or noisy and quiet areas.

4. Cupboards should be used to develop variety in height, colour, and texture around the room. Try to use the cupboards and shelves in interesting ways to distinguish one area from another, as well as to provide appropriate storage space at each centre.

5. When arranging centres, keep space open for easy traffic flow from centre to centre, from each centre to the door, from each centre to the large group meeting area, and from each centre to the bathroom.

6. Keep in mind that an adult standing in any part of the room should be able to note children in each centre around the room.

Figure 1-4

Organizing, Displaying, Setting Out Equipment and Materials

Materials related to subject areas should be organized into cupboard spaces at the most appropriate centres. This does not mean that the materials are only used at that centre, but it does ease location and access to them when needed. Clearly labelled boxes such as shoe boxes, chocolate boxes, file folder boxes, or coffee cans with plastic lids can be arranged according to size and shape to create neatness and easy access.

The way in which I set out equipment and materials plays an important role in developing each child's self esteem and sense of order in the world, and in maintaining my own organization in planning. At each centre, tools, materials, and equipment are set out in an orderly and inviting arrangement before the children arrive. These are arranged so they can be easily seen and reached by the children who choose to go to that centre.

I believe children's self esteem is heightened if materials look as though they are placed there especially for each individual. This means that the centre should have the distinct look of being 'set' for whoever chooses to go there. This idea also aids in developing cooperation and responsibility as children are encouraged at cleanup time, to tidy the centre and to replace used materials, so that the centre may look inviting to someone else. To facilitate this, replacement materials should always be in easy access to each centre. If this is encouraged from the beginning of the year, the children should be quite considerate and adept at 'setting' centres for others very early in the year.

Dealing with materials which create a lot of noise in the classroom is often a problem. By lowering noise levels, we can help ourselves to be more relaxed teachers, as well as provide the children with a more relaxed and tension-reduced environment. See Figure 1-5 for ways that have helped me create a quieter classroom atmosphere.

My Suggestions For Teachers

1. The noise of pots and pans against wooden or metal cupboards in the Housekeeping Centre can be toned down by lining shelves and drawers with felt. I also like to place felt circles on the stove burners in this centre.

2. Blocks in the Block Centre can create loud clunking sounds as the children place them back on the shelves at cleanup time. The best way to muffle these noises is to line cupboard shelves (sides, top, bottom) with carpeting.

3. When hard objects are stored in cans (e.g., marbles) 'sharp' noises can be alleviated by gluing felt pads on the bottom of each can or lining the inside bottom and sides with felt or carpet.

4. A felt tablecloth or blotter-type paper placed on a table may help to muffle the sharp noises of small hard objects being dropped during manipulation.

Figure 1-5

Conclusion

The classroom environment reflects the atmosphere generated by those who are within. The physical arrangement of space and things also reflects the kind of environment that prevails in the classroom. As teachers, we can do a lot to promote a warm and caring environment through the way in which we interact with others and through the way in which we consider people when planning and arranging physical space.

Introduction

In the development of an effective early childhood program, I have found that long range planning is the most important step. It reflects the structure of the learning environment. When this basic organizational pattern of the program has been established, shorter term plans are more effective because a general direction has been set. Long range planning follows the general developmental levels, learning patterns, and interests of young children. Though it is the most tentative, I still consider it the most important initial step to planning any program.

The first section of this chapter discusses important considerations to be made when doing long range planning. These discussions focus on the structuring of the learning environment, and the learning patterns and play interests of young children.

The second section of this chapter is a general overview of the underlying goals of my early childhood program. This overview is an important step in developing an idea of your own philosophy of what is important, on the basis of what you know about child development, learning behaviours, and characteristics of young children. I have found that by developing an idea of what my basic beliefs are, I can more easily move from generally stated goals to more specific long range plans.

The last section of this chapter provides a completed format which illustrates how I move from general to more specific goals. A blank format, which is useful for sequencing experiences and materials, is also provided.

Planning

Structuring the Learning Environment

The long range plan serves as an underlying structure that states the tentative progression of content in the program. This structure facilitates the organization of content to be presented to the children. It does not stifle creativity and thought and is not felt by the child nor seen by the casual observer.

Structuring the learning environment so that it progresses along with children's growth and development depends on the teacher's ability to apply what is known about child development, learning patterns, and interests of young children to what is known about different kinds of play and play materials. The teacher must relate the level of child development to the possibilities of play with different materials and the educational value of that play. An example follows:

<u>Child's Level of Development</u>   Preoperational Stage
- children develop an understanding of others in their world best through imaginative play

<u>Activity and Materials</u>
- play with dressup clothes and costumes
- play 'home' activity with child-sized furniture, dolls, and accessories such as pots and pans, dishes, brooms, mops, telephones, mirrors, etc.

<u>Educational Value</u>
- child initiated dramatic play of adult, child, and fantasy roles
- emotional satisfaction through the use of fantasy
- communication of ideas through interacting with others
- reproduction of real life roles

Early childhood program structure which reflects knowledge of child development, play, and materials is evident by the order in which activities and materials are to be presented, and by the order in which concepts and skills are to be introduced. An example of how activities and materials may be sequenced from simple exploration to the development of more complex concepts in long range planning is seen in Figure 2-1. Figure 2-2 demonstrates how ideas from three different times (September 20, January 12, and April 18) during the school year (taken from Figure 2-1) may be expanded in the daily planning.

Figure 2-1

September 20   Sand Centre

<u>Objective</u>   To explore properties of sand
<u>Activity</u>   Introduce dry sand and containers for pouring and holding sand
<u>Concepts and Skills</u>   Awareness that sand is made up of small grains and that sand flows when dry

January 12   Sand Centre

<u>Objective</u>   To develop an awareness of how balance scales work
<u>Activity</u>   Introduce dry sand and various sized containers (bags, cans), and balance scale
<u>Concepts and Skills</u>   Comparing weights and concept of heavy/light, heavier/lighter

April 18   Sand Centre

<u>Objective</u>   To explore and compare weights of wet and dry sand
<u>Activity</u>   Divide sand in the sand table with a small board (one side dry sand, one side wet sand), then provide each child with a balance scale and two identical containers for the comparison of dry and wet sand
<u>Concepts and Skills</u>   Awareness of differences in properties of wet and dry sand

Figure 2-2

Characteristics of young children provide many clues helpful to structuring the learning environment of the young child. The following section discusses learning patterns and general characteristics of children between the ages of five and seven years.

Learning Patterns of Young Children

Jean Piaget's theory of intellectual development proposes that intelligence develops in a sequence of stages. According to this theory, the children we interact with (ages five to seven years) are mainly in the last part of the preoperational stage, in transition from the preoperational to the concrete, or just entering the concrete stage of development.

These characteristics of children do influence program planning and careful note must be taken of them. Some of the major principles underlying the development of children at these ages are discussed here:

1. Children are naturally active and play is essential to their intellectual growth.

As teachers of young children who learn best through concrete experiences and play, we must keep in mind a statement by Marianne Parry (1976) in her book, *From Two To Five*. She says that "There are two levels of play, one which merely keeps children occupied, the other which contributes to their educational development (page 19)." Therefore, we must be considerate of the materials we present to children, we must watch for progression in play, and we must know when to provide more materials, or when to intervene in the play to keep it from becoming idle.

2. Children's thinking processes are different from those of adults.

I was reminded of this during a visit to a school when a teacher was telling the children that the goldfish had died. The teacher said, "I have some sad news for you. One of our fish died again." One little boy asked, "When did it die before?" Sad to say, the little boy's question went unanswered and his puzzled expression went unnoticed. Children take adults literally, therefore, we must be careful about the way we speak. Implications for the way we interact with children arise from this characteristic.

We must also be very clear about what we mean when we are talking to young children. For example in another classroom, all of the phrases used by a teacher over a two-hour period, which meant "be more quiet" were noted. These were, "My head h-u-r-t-s", "I'm w-a-i-t-i-n-g", "I'm not h-a-p-p-y", "Excuse me, do I have to remind you about you know what?" Young children interpret the words they hear in terms of their background experiences. If a message seems confusing, it is because children have not been able to apply what they already know to help them make sense of the message. If children are presented with a variety of messages, all meaning the same thing, they must first try to interpret the message when it occurs, and then follow the instruction. We must be considerate of young children's unique background and unpolished facility when we interpret their words and phrases.

3. Children learn better through concrete representations than through abstract propositions at this age.

Children must experience the real object or event simultaneously with verbal information about it. They are interested in the 'here and now', and will not perceive abstract ideas until they have developed a store of background knowledge from many concrete experiences. Mistaken ideas about such things as Inuit, igloos, dinosaurs, etc., may develop if children are presented with them before they have developed basic conceptual frameworks on which to hang these new ideas.

These major characteristics help to establish a link between how children learn and their interests. Our belief that children express interests in various ways through the vehicle of play is confirmed in the examples of actual quotes from children, which appear in the following section.

Play and Interests of Young Children

Play activities are serious business to young children. Through play children can express their own unique interests in activities. Play is children's way of exploring, experimenting, building relations between ideas, and discovering how to come to terms with their world, and to cope with the real world.

Children satisfy needs through expressing their interests in play. I have found that each child is a unique individual with a unique personality who has unique likes and dislikes. When children are allowed to choose tasks of their own interest, they seem to be more motivated, self directed, and exhibit feelings of self worth. In order to determine play preferences and interests of young children, I interviewed twenty children between five and nine years of age individually. I asked each child, "What kinds of things are you most interested in doing when you play?" The following responses confirm my belief that children do express their interests and their needs in various ways while they play. These statements also provide many clues about young children and have implications for planning.

Clue   Young children seek warmth and security in relationships with people and animals.

Implications for Planning   Program plans must reflect each child's need for acceptance, to be loved, to be treated gently, and to experience positive relationships. Theme plans which may help to develop these feelings are: "Kindness and Consideration", "Myself and Others", or "Care for Living Things".

Make books because that's my favourite thing because I like to write and draw too.
(6 years)

I like typing letters to my friend, that is if I can use the typewriter.
(6 years)

Listening to stories is the best thing to do because you [teacher] can do it like read a story, and my mom or dad can do it too, and I can listen. Even, my dad lets me turn the pages.
(5 years)

I like to do quiet reading because I like to do reading with Buffy, my hamster, on my tummy.
(8 years)

I like to play with lego. I can build things when I want, and take them apart when I want.
(5 years)

I like to wash dishes in the sink 'cause it's like at the water table, and my brother can put them away. It's fun to make bubbles on my arms all the way up to my sleeves.
(7 years)

I like building things out of sand because if they fall, I can build something else.
(5 years)

Clue Young children learn through and enjoy imaginative play.

Implications for Planning   Children need opportunities to develop understandings of the world in which they live, and to gain confidence in themselves through imaginative play. Careful consideration to materials which will stimulate this kind of play, adequate space for the child to play in, and time in which play can develop are necessary. For example, one long block of time in which play can occur is more conducive to the development of imaginative play than two or more shorter blocks of time.

Clue Young children are in a stage of rapid development of language, and are fascinated by print.

Implications for Planning   These play preferences of children give us clues for developing many ideas which may be included as daily centre activities in theme plans. Activities like the following might be provided:

- Opportunities for children to state their interpretations of ideas and to see them being recorded, then go over them later so they also experience the ideas as stored information. For example, "My mother made a snow-suit for my Cabbage Patch doll."
- Opportunities for children to make their own books at their own level (e.g., drawing, scribbling, copying printed words, etc.).
- Opportunities for children to hear stories which have been chosen by them, as well as those you have chosen on the basis of your observations to extend understandings.
- Opportunities for children to use typewriters at the Writing Centre.
- Opportunities for children to have access to soft toys or dolls to be cuddled and held while they look at books or read.

I like to sit on the step and think and watch and think about things, and think about somebody or think about riding my bike.
(7 years)

Sometimes I like to just hang around and look at a book — like not talk to anyone, just look at books.
(7 years)

Clue Young children need space and time to be alone.

Implications for Planning   Young children need time to be alone and space where they can retreat from others. A quiet corner, cushions, soft chairs, and stuffed toys can help to create the environment in which children may find security and comfort when they seek it.

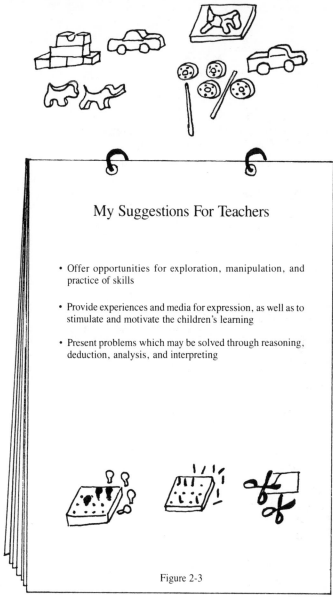

Clue Young children are curious about the world.

Implication for Planning The child's natural interest in wanting in explore and find out, his questions, and need for explanations must be capitalized on through providing many progressive activities which present scientific principles and characteristics of things. Often these activities may be introduced following a child's spontaneous question or comment, or following the reading of a book in which a scientific principle is presented in a simple way. For example, the story *Mr. Archimede's Bath* (Allen, 1980) may motivate an interest in the displacement of water by a solid. When the teacher provides natural materials or stories of interest for a particular age group, the children's natural curiosity will motivate them to explore and find out for themselves.

Planning is the key to an effective, well organized early childhood program which corresponds with each child's development. The content of the program must be structured according to the development of young children and in concert with their learning patterns and interests. The following section is a broad overview of the underlying goals of the early childhood program which I teach. This overview may help to support some of the notions just presented.

Underlying Goals of an Early Childhood Program

The underlying goals of an early childhood program are determined by consideration of developmental stages, learning behaviors, and characteristics of young children. Following is a broad overview of what I believe are the major underlying goals of an early childhood program.

To foster motivation for learning

The classroom environment must be structured by the selection of media, apparatus, and tools, and these should be arranged before the children arrive, to focus their attention and interest. I find the criteria in Figure 2-3 helpful when considering choice of materials and activities.

To develop personality and social awareness

A positive and stable self concept is essential to the child's adjustment, both to himself and to others. Children form ideas about themselves in relation to the people in their environment. If children feel accepted, they accept themselves, and have the confidence to make decisions and be self reliant.

Experiences and activities should be provided which will help to create a warm, caring atmosphere in the classroom. Children must be helped to adapt to the larger sphere of the school group and to create a balanced sense of order and freedom.

Children learn about their environment through observation, firsthand experiences, and discovery. Through discussion and sharing they can be encouraged to talk about what is important to them and to listen to each other. Consideration for the rights of others may develop through many of the classroom routines such as sharing materials, making choices, waiting for a turn at an activity and cleaning up.

Cooperative activities at centres such as Sand, Block, Home, Water, etc., must be provided with appropriate material to stimulate dramatic play. This will enable the children to communicate effectively with each other, while contributing to their social growth and understanding.

To develop sensory awareness

Learning and sensory experiences go hand in hand and are dependent on one another. Therefore, experiences and activities should be provided which assist the children's modifying perceptions of the environment as they grow and learn, which may help them to categorize and which make sense of impressions. I find the activities listed on Figure 2-4 help to develop children's sensory awareness.

My Suggestions For Teachers

1. Look at colours, colour differences, shapes, spaces between shapes, and at textures

2. Listen to and identify a variety of sounds and tones that are high or low

3. Touch rough, smooth, warm, cold surfaces, feel sensations such as finger painting, or paint with pudding

4. Smell and identify sharp, sweet, strong, or faint smells

5. Taste and identify bland, salty, or sweet sensations

Figure 2-4

Through the provision of appropriate language, the process of learning that things have different distinctive features can be enhanced, and the children may more easily express understandings about unique characteristics that differentiate some things from other things.

To build concepts

The concepts children develop are influenced by the society in which they live as well as through well thought-out, progressive and sequential activities planned by the teacher. Activities must be planned to encourage children to find significant patterns in their environment, to develop new ideas, and to relate present ideas to concepts being developed. Sequential activities should be devised to provide appropriately challenging opportunities for the children to be involved in observation, comparison, construction with apparatus, and manipulation of materials. Through these activities, children will become more familiar with basic scientific principles and characteristics of things in their environment.

Children's inquisitive nature and intrinsic need to master new situations must be considered in the provision of activities. Activities in classifying, grouping, seriation, spatial relationships, patterning, and development of an awareness of similarities and differences will provide the basis for the formation of mathematical and scientific concepts. Children are particularly interested in quantitative gradations of things, and are usually preoccupied with who has more or less. Repetition of stories such as "The Three Bears" or "The Three Billy Goats Gruff" are enjoyed by children while at the same time help to undergird their mathematical reasoning.

Children's experiences can be extended as they learn to sort, match, sequence, compute, balance, and weigh, as they are guided to define the function of things, and as they are led to an interest in measuring and counting. Children's desire to experiment and their thrill in discovery is capitalized on as they identify properties of natural elements such as snow, air, water, dirt, sand, or rain. This also becomes evident as they test out their skill in cooking.

Together with these activities, children should be encouraged to build language to describe their experiences.

They must be encouraged to record their experiences in pictures, through dictation, or through their own attempts at writing words. A developing ability to associate symbols with concepts helps to provide the means for dealing with later abstractions.

To provide for growth in vocabulary and fluency in language

Each child's desire to communicate ideas, feelings, and problems must be facilitated through a variety of experiences. Each child should learn to sequence events, select appropriate and meaningful words, and convey messages with increasing power through talking and sharing with an adult who may record on experience charts, or write words dictated by the child. Pocket chart, typewriter, flannel board,

or chalkboard activities can be available for children to try out words, to play with sentence patterns, poetry, and story patterns, to connect the printed word with ideas, and to develop a sense of how language works. Have blank booklets of varied shapes and sizes available at many locations in the classroom to facilitate the child's spontaneous desire to record ideas.

Through hearing stories, poems, and watching films, as well as through discussions and writing, children develop ability in predicting and interpreting. Facilitation through activities and encouragement of the developing interest in print is an essential function of the early reading and early writing process.

The children's power over language may also be enhanced by listening to stories, poetry, records, watching films, and filmstrips, and by joining in finger plays and singing games as a shared group activity. Consideration must be given to experiences the children have had, their familiarity with the topic, or the need to stimulate interest in new experiences when choosing appropriate activities.

To foster creative and imaginative expression

We must preserve the child's untarnished view of the world and encourage creativity through supporting expressions of individuality. Through a choice of materials and activities that will arouse aesthetic pleasure, motivate sensory investigation, and develop visual forms of creative expressions, the child's individuality may be encouraged and valued.

Musical instruments at the Music Centre encourage children to experiment, manipulate, and compose their own tunes. Dress up clothing and other props provided in the Home Centre help elicit spontaneous understandings through dramatic play as children act out their feelings and ideas.

Materials in the Block, Sand, Water, and Art centres help in developing creativity with ideas through cooperative efforts, and may provide opportunities for planning, organization, and the building of relations between play material and experiences in the child's real world.

To develop physical coordination and control

Gross motor development is encouraged both in the classroom and in the gymnasium through opportunities to explore the physical environment, gain mastery of body skills, and coordinate actions through spontaneous free movement. The outdoor play area invites children to involve themselves in self directed activity and develop an awareness of spatial relations.

Within the classroom, many activities lead to the use and control of small muscles and coordination of fingers and eyes. Children are easily motivated by their natural desire to achieve control of tools such as felt markers, pencils, paint brushes, needles, and woodworking tools. The manipulation required to fit pieces into puzzles, thread beads, cut shapes, paste, or tie shoes helps to encourage the development of fine motor skills.

17

Musical activities in which children interpret the pattern to their own movements of rocking, swaying, skipping, galloping, trotting, and clapping help to develop rhythm. Balance and coordination are gained by the children's combined movements with a parachute and by the use of various equipment such as balance beams, hoops, and ropes to walk on, around, or through.

Structuring the content in an early childhood program is best achieved by first developing an idea of what you feel is important on the basis of the children's levels of development, learning patterns, and interests. Then, experiences and materials should be sequenced so that they follow a progression from simple to more complex, consistent with the child's development. The next section provides information which may be helpful in planning progression in the program.

Sequencing Experiences and Materials in an Integrated Program

The range of developmental levels of children in an early childhood program, together with the vast array or dearth of materials available often become the root of confusion in program planning. The format I find most useful in ensuring a sequential ordering of opportunities to develop concepts and skills is shown in Figures 2-5 and 2-6. Using this format helps to ensure variety as well as exposure to a wide range of experiences. A blank format (see Figure 2-5), as well as a completed sample (see Figure 2-6) are provided. These may assist or extend your own ideas in the development of scope and sequence for each of the centres.

Conclusion

Long range planning establishes a strong base on which to build an early childhood program. When making long range plans we must take into account what we know about child development, learning behaviours, and interests of young children. Long range plans must be tentative but even in their tentative state they do provide a lot of guidance to theme and daily planning.

When planning themes, consideration is given to the unique characteristics of each child's learning and development as well as to the progression set out in the long range plan. Chapter Three will discuss the importance of theme planning and provide guidance for developing a theme plan.

September	October	November
December	January	February
March	April	May
June		

Figure 2-5

Carpentry

September	October	November
Closed	Closed	Closed Open on second week · Children to glue scraps of wood, cloth, and styrofoam together.
December · Children to paint structures made from wood, cloth, and styrofoam scraps glued together. · Children to construct a Christmas gift.	January · Introduce hammer and large-headed nails, and stamps of wood. · Children to pound nails into the wood, and to pull them out with claw of hammer. · Introduce small pieces of wood, styrofoam, and cloth. Children to construct using hammer and nails.	February · Introduce sand paper. Children to sand structures. · Introduce tape measures. · Introduce the idea of making plans. Children to make plans for structures they plan to build. · Introduce large pieces of soft wood for children to nail together.
March · Emphasize making plans before constructing. · Introduce saw and vise. · Children to cut soft wood with saw, to use in constructions. · Introduce rasp and round file to smooth rough edges.	April · Introduce blank booklets for children to draw plans, completed structures, and to write words in. · Introduce hand drills. · Introduce screws and screwdrivers. · Emphasize planning, building, and writing about structure.	May · Move Carpentry Centre outdoors on nice days. · All equipment previously introduced should be available for use. · Encourage children to write about their constructions in blank booklets.

June
· Continue as in May.
· Encourage children to complete activity sequence in the following order:
  · Plan
  · Construct/Paint
  · Write		

Figure 2-6

18

Introduction

Theme planning in this book refers to the planning which focuses on a predetermined topic. The topic is evident in each of the activities provided for the children. The importance of careful and thorough theme planning cannot be over emphasized. I give careful consideration to the needs, interests, and abilities of each child as well as to the broad goals set out in the long range plan. My main aim in planning a theme is to create a well ordered environment in which children are motivated and self directed in their activities. Again, I find that I learn about children's interests and needs from the statements made by the children themselves. For example, the following statements made during interviews reflect the diversity of interests that are typical of children in their early years:

> I like the quiet at silent reading time. You can read but you can think about other things also.
> (8 years)

> I like to do art because it's fun because you get to paint, and you get to experiment with things.
> (6 years)

> Centre time is the best time because you can do the thing you want to, like going to the Hospital Centre or going to the Writing Centre, or going to the quiet Reading Centre.
> (5 years)

Most research supports the idea that for young children, learning is often a social activity in which they need to discuss experiences and interests with one another within small groups. Individual interests can be fostered and catered to in small groups, where children work as individuals in a self directed way, and then interact with others whose interests are similar.

Planning according to thematic units helps the teacher to more easily provide for the range in children's needs, interests, and abilities. The theme topic provides a common thread between activities and helps to make the integrated centre approach possible. A simple example of an initial step in planning for integrated centres is seen in Figure 3-1. This shows how the theme is the central focus and how consideration may be given to each of the centres to determine what, if any, activity can be provided at particular centres. It is important to keep in mind that as well as relating the theme of Nursery Rhymes to each centre, each activity must be suitable to the children's level of learning.

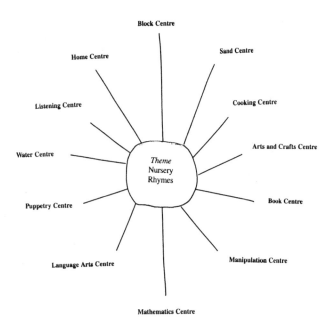

Figure 3-1

Themes

"Theme" is a term which I use as a label for a topic around which the program is planned. The topic may be introduced through a real experience (e.g., field trip) or through a vicarious experience (e.g., film, pictures). Themes may be planned around almost any topic of interest to the children. Some examples of themes generally of interest to young children between five and seven or eight years, and commonly used in early childhood programs are topics such as "Me as an Individual" and "Colours and Shapes" used in the first term, and "Wind and Kites" used in the spring. Themes are often very broad ideas which may be more manageable if divided into units, for example:

Theme   Me As An Individual

Unit One   Characteristics of Me

Unit Two   My Feelings

Theme planning helps in maintaining linkages between activities. Themes also help children to make connections between ideas. For example, the theme "Nursery Rhymes"

(see Figure 3-1) can be experienced in many different contexts within the classroom and at many different centres (i.e., Sand, Water, Home, Block, Art, etc.). Different experiences, at different centres all based on the same topic, provide opportunities for the children to think about the same thing in different ways. For example in a theme on "Colours and Shapes", the children may learn about primary colours and shapes in different ways at different centres. At the Block Centre a variety of red, yellow, and blue blocks of different shapes are provided and are to be matched to sheets of red, blue, and yellow construction paper. At the Home Centre, paper plates, onto which different shapes of white tissue paper are stapled, are used as blotters onto which drops of red, blue, and yellow coloured water are dropped.

Many different formats are available for theme planning. Following is a format which works well for me:

Theme Format

Title
Tentative time frame

Major objectives
Related objectives

Motivation

Real Experiences e.g., field trips, resource visitors
Vicarious Experiences e.g., films, displays, stories

Large group activities

For example, group work, discussions, stories, poems, fingerplays, songs, games, etc.

Discussion topics

Integration of the theme into centres

List each centre separately and list activities and materials planned for each particular centre
List concepts and skills to be developed for each activity

Culminating activity

List ways in which all learning may be brought together to a conclusion e.g., special day, displays, performances, etc.

Evaluation

Observations, checklists, etc.

Resource Materials

List teacher and student references, library books, films, filmstrips, records, pictures, curriculum resources, etc.

Diagraming may be used to ensure integration of the theme into different centres and activities and to ensure that different experiences at different centres are all related to the topic of the theme. Figures 3-2 and 3-3 show examples of basic diagraming for the themes "Nursery Rhymes" and "Kindness and Consideration". Ideas are inserted where applicable and centres not appropriate to development of the theme are crossed out.

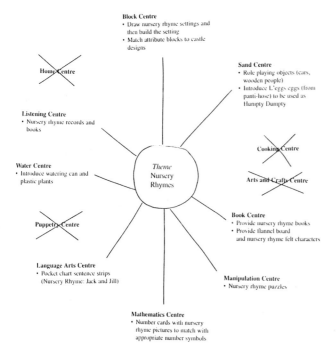

Figure 3-2

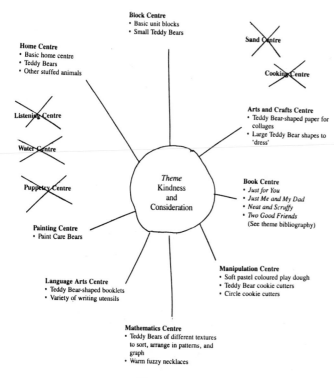

Figure 3-3

An Expanded Theme Plan

Introduction

The following plan on the theme "Kindness and Consideration" is suitable for use early in the year as it helps to set the tone of the classroom by developing feelings of kindness, empathy, and sympathy. When this theme focuses on fantasy characters of young children (e.g., Care Bears) it provides a base on which further social and emotional growth can be encouraged throughout the year.

When this theme is introduced early in the year, the theme idea can flow throughout the entire year. I have used the "Care Bear" as a symbol of my program by using Care Bear characters in the following ways:

- as juice 'tickets' at the juice table (see Figure 3-4)
- as birthday bears (see Figure 3-4)
- as bear-shaped books for children to write in throughout the year
- as bear-shaped paper at the Art or Paint Centre
- as shapes of, or outlines around reminders and notes to parents
- as sand bag shapes
- as puppet shapes

As the theme is being planned, it is important to keep the time frame in mind and to be selective about activities chosen.

Theme Plan

Title   Kindness and Consideration

Tentative time frame   September 15-30

Major objectives

- To develop a base on which to establish an atmosphere of warmth and caring
- To develop feelings of kindness and consideration toward one another.

Related Objectives

- To create an awareness of feelings of self
- To create an awareness of feelings of others
- To develop empathy for how others feel
- To develop care and trust in one another

21

Motivation

Talk about Care Bears, to find out what the children already know about them. Show pictures of Care Bears and read a story about them (e.g., *A Tale From the Care Bears, A Sister For Sam,* Mason, 1983).

Note   The following ideas are introduced at this time but will be ongoing throughout the year:
- Introduce the birthday Care Bear bulletin board display, which has been prepared ahead of time with Care Bears depicting individual birthdays displayed on appropriate cloud shapes for each month.
- Introduce Care Bear birthday hats which children may wear and take home on their birthdays.

Talk about Warm Fuzzies and Cold Pricklies to find out what the children know about them. Then tell the Warm

Fuzzy Story (see "A Story to Tell About Kindness" in Resource Materials).

Large Group Activities

Discussions (see discussion topics listed in next section)

Stories (see book list in Resource Materials)

Finger plays, Verses, and Songs (see Resource Materials)

Creative Movement Activities

After the children have developed a familiarity with what Warm Fuzzies and Cold Pricklies are, they may be encouraged to dig the imaginary Cold Pricklies out of their pockets and to throw them away. Then they may be encouraged to fill their pockets with imaginary Warm Fuzzies.

The children may also be encouraged to do creative movement around the classroom as they listen to music. Suggested music for creative movement in the "Kindness and Consideration" theme is "It's a Small World" (Sharon, Lois, and Bram, 1981). Suggestions can also be made for the

children to move like happy Care Bears, sad Care Bears, Warm Fuzzies, Cold Pricklies, a happy person, a kind person, a considerate person, a sad person, etc.

Juice Bear

Birthday Bear

Care Bears

Cut bears from coloured construction paper and use felt markers to fill in the details like the eyes, nose, etc. Cut the "cloud tummies" from white paper and paste on the figure of the bear.

Figure 3-4

Discussion Topics

- <u>Kindness</u> Encourage talk about what it means to be kind, ways to be kind, or times when they were kind
- <u>Consideration</u> Encourage talk about what it means to be considerate, ways to be considerate, or times when the children have been considerate
- <u>Ways to be nice to each other in a classroom</u>
- <u>Care Bear stories after they have been read</u>
- <u>Warm Fuzzies and Cold Pricklies after they have been introduced</u>

<u>Note</u> It is important for the children to have some knowledge about the topic before expecting them to discuss it. While discussing topics, most of the talk should be done by the children, with the teacher acting as facilitator and respondent of talk.

Integration of the Theme into Learning Centres

Be selective in choosing activities based on your chosen theme topic, and keep in mind the time frame you have set for the theme.

The following centre activities cover the two-week period of the theme. In order to show the progression from simple to more complex, basic materials are presented in week one, and supplementary or additional materials are presented in week two. Concepts and skills to be developed through the materials and activities are also given.

Centre Activities

Concepts/Skills to be developed

Juice Centre

Week One

Introduce juice Care Bears (see Figure 3-4) which may be used as juice tickets by the children at this centre any time during the regular centre time. Children must put the tickets into a container on the table when the juice is taken, then they must sit down to drink their juice. Only four children are allowed at this centre at one time.

Consideration for others
Classroom routines
Early reading
Counting
One-to-one relationships

Home Centre

Week One

Provide basic Home Centre materials and equipment

Role playing and dramatization
Sharing materials

Week Two

Introduce Teddy Bears, and other stuffed animals as supplementary material.

Kindness and consideration
Role playing and dramatization
Self expression
Social skills in interpersonal
  communications

Block Centre		**Concepts/Skills Which May Be Developed**

Week One

Basic unit blocks

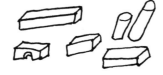

Sharing
Awareness of attributes of blocks
Role playing
Expressive skills

Week Two

Children to build homes for small Teddy Bears or other stuffed animals.

Kindness and consideration
Sharing
Awareness of attributes of blocks
Role playing
Social and expressive skills

Sand Centre

Week One

Provide three Teddy Bear-shaped sand bags of different sizes (see Figure 3-5 in Resource Materials for pattern).

Physical properties of sand
Weight and size concepts

Week Two

Provide two more Teddy Bear-shaped sand bags (sizes to fit in with seriated sizes presented in Week One).

Sequencing or ordering
Comparing weight and sizes

Arts and Crafts Centre

Week One

Teddy Bear-shaped paper, glue, and a variety of materials to make a collage.

Texture awareness
Shape awareness
Creativity
Vocabulary related to texture and shapes

Week Two

Large Teddy Bear shapes, glue and sheets of tissue paper. Children to cut clothing from tissue paper to dress their Teddy Bears.

Shape awareness
Creativity
Vocabulary related to pieces

Manipulation Centre

Week One

Provide soft, pastel coloured playdough, rolling pins, Teddy Bear and circle-shaped cookie cutters.

(This centre is not open in Week Two)

Creativity
Self expression
Sharing
Shape awareness

Painting Centre

(This centre is not open in Week One)

Week Two

Encourage children to paint Care Bears, Care Bear clouds, Warm Fuzzies, and Cold Pricklies, people being kind, people being considerate, etc.

Creativity
Self expression
Early writing

Mathematics Centre

Week One

Classify Teddy Bear shapes of different textures. Count the number of each different texture.

Classification
Texture awareness
Counting one-to-one

Week Two

Make Warm Fuzzy necklaces (see Figure 3-6 in Resource Materials for pattern).

Space/shapes

Language Arts Centre

Weeks One and Two

Children to draw and write in Teddy Bear-shaped booklets using a variety of writing utensils (pencils, fine felt markers, crayons and chalk).

Early writing
Early reading
Manipulation
Sharing
Expressive skills

Quiet Reading Centre

Weeks One and Two

Provide books in the quiet Reading Centre which relate to the theme "Kindness and Consideration" (See Resource Materials for a list of children's books).

Culminating Activities

Hold a Teddy Bear Day. Send a note to parents, on Teddy Bear-shaped paper, announcing that children may bring their Teddy Bears to school. Since some children may not have Teddy Bears, let them know that any stuffed animal or doll is appropriate. I also like to have Teddy Bears from the Home Centre available, as well as to bring some from home. Ask for volunteers to make Teddy Bear-shaped jello pieces, Teddy Bear-shaped cookies, and to draw Teddy Bears on styrofoam juice cups. Have each child introduce and talk about his Teddy Bear. I have found that if the children introduce their Teddy Bears in small groups, there is less chance of them becoming bored (as they might in large group introduction sessions).

Evaluation of Learning Centres

Immediately after centre time, I like to choose four or five children to share and talk about the centre they have participated at that day and find it useful to record the names of the children each day. Keeping a record helps to ensure that each child gets a turn to share his ideas at least once every few days. I try to encourage each child to talk freely, with as little prompting from me as possible.

Resource Materials

Books

Delton, Judy. *Two Good Friends*. New York: Crown Publishers, Inc., 1974.

Elkind, David. *The Hurried Child*. Don Mills, Ontario: Addision-Wesley Publishing Company, 1981.

Flemming, Bonnie M., and Hamilton, Darlene S. *Resources for Creative Teaching in Early Childhood Education*. New York: Harcourt Brace Jovanovich, Inc., 1977.

Flint Board of Education. *Ring a Ring O Roses*. Flint, Michigan: Flint Board of Education, 1981.

Freed, A. *T.A. For Tots, Vol. 11*. Sacramento, California: Jalmar Press Ind., 1980.

Gale, Jennifer. *Neat and Scruffy*. Ashton Scholastic, 1976.

Manning, K. and Sharp, A. *Structuring Play*. London: Ward Lock Educational, 1980.

Mayer, Mercer. *Just For You*. New York: Golden Press, 1975.

_____. *Just Grandma and Me*. New York: Western Publishing Company, Inc., 1983.

_____. *Just Me and My Dad*. New York: Golden Press, 1977.

Ross, Dave. *A Book of Hugs*. New York: Thomas Y. Crowell, 1980.

Silverstein, Shel. *The Missing Piece*. New York: Harper and Row Publishers, 1976.

Fingerplays, Songs and Verses

Teddy Bear (action verse)
Teddy Bear, Teddy Bear
Turn around.
Teddy Bear, Teddy Bear
Touch the ground.
Teddy Bear, Teddy Bear
Show your shoe.
Teddy Bear, Teddy Bear
I love you.
Teddy Bear, Teddy Bear
Climb the stairs.
Teddy Bear, Teddy Bear
Say your prayers.
Teddy Bear, Teddy Bear
Say good night.

Good Manners (verse)
We say thank you,
We say please.
We don't interrupt or tease.
We don't argue,
We don't fuss,
We listen when you talk to us.

My Friends (action verse)
My friends are nicely smiling, smiling, smiling.
My friends are nicely smiling,
And I will smile at them.
(Repeat, substituting the following actions:
politely bowing, gaily waving, gently nodding.
Encourage the children to think of other actions.)

Two Little Friends (fingerplay)
Two little friends are better than one (hold up two fingers)
And three are better than two (hold up three fingers)
And four are much better still (hold up four fingers).
Just think!
What four little friends can do (wiggle four fingers).

If You're Happy and You Know It (song)
If you're happy and you know it,
Clap your hands.
If you're happy and you know it,
Clap your hands.
If you're happy and you know it,
Then your face will surely show it.
If you're happy and you know it,
Clap your hands.
(Repeat, substituting the following action:
stamp your feet, nod your head, do all three.
Encourage the children to think of other actions.)

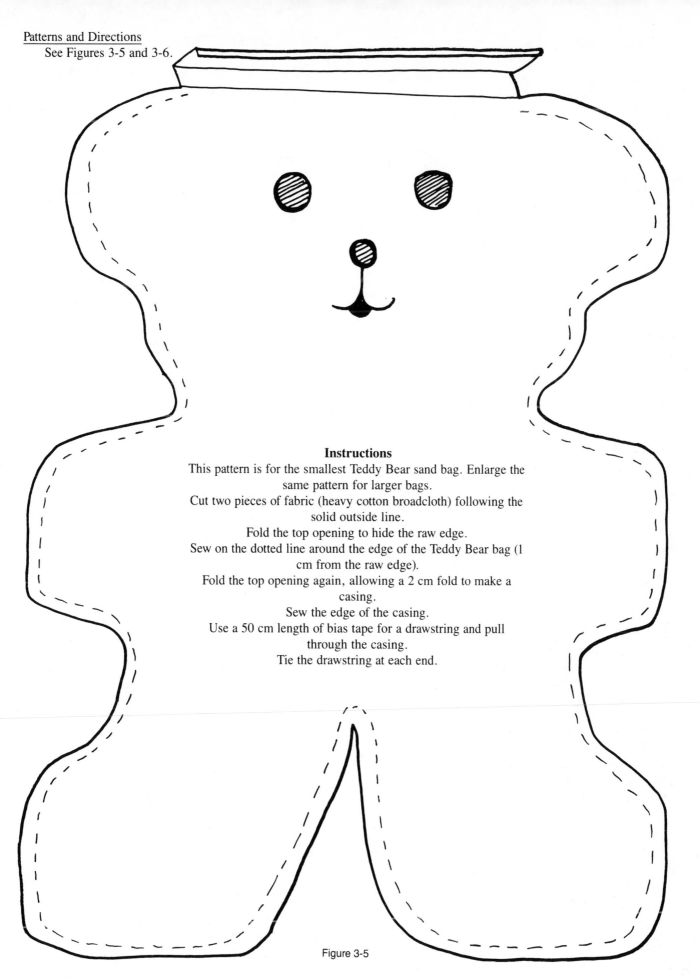

Instructions

This pattern is for the smallest Teddy Bear sand bag. Enlarge the same pattern for larger bags.

Cut two pieces of fabric (heavy cotton broadcloth) following the solid outside line.

Fold the top opening to hide the raw edge.

Sew on the dotted line around the edge of the Teddy Bear bag (1 cm from the raw edge).

Fold the top opening again, allowing a 2 cm fold to make a casing.

Sew the edge of the casing.

Use a 50 cm length of bias tape for a drawstring and pull through the casing.

Tie the drawstring at each end.

Figure 3-5

Materials

Yarn, scissors, and lightweight cardboard.

Procedure

Cut two circular pieces of cardboard, approximately 5 cm in diameter. Cut a 2 cm diameter hole in the middle of both circles.

e.g.,

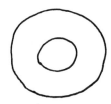

Place the circles together (like a sandwich). Wind approximately 2 metre lengths of yarn around and around the circles until no cardboard is visible through the yarn.

e.g.,

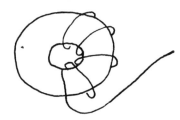

Hold the circle firmly at the middle. Cut the yarn on the outside edge, keeping the yarn on the cardboard circle.

e.g.,

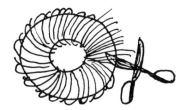

Tie a 1 metre length of yarn firmly around the inside circle (between the two circles of cardboard). Once firmly tied, tie the ends of the yarn together. Remove the cardboard circles from the yarn ball. Glue on paper or fabric eyes.

Figure 3-6

Stories

A Story to Tell About Kindness

Once upon a time there was a tiny village where everyone was happy. No one frowned or grumbled. Everybody just smiled, said nice things, and did kind things for one another.

Everybody in that village carried around bags of Warm Fuzzies. These Warm Fuzzies were nice things they could do for others. Whenever anyone wanted to do something nice, all they had to do was reach into their bag and pull out a Warm Fuzzy. Sometimes it was a smile, and sometimes it was a kind word. There were all kinds of nice things in those Warm Fuzzy bags.

One day a bad witch came to visit the village. She was always growling and only liked people to be grumpy and sad. She did not like the happy village one bit, and especially did not like to see people carrying Warm Fuzzy bags and giving Warm Fuzzies to everyone. The witch decided she would make everyone stop giving away Warm Fuzzies.

The bad witch thought about what she could do to make the people stop giving away Warm Fuzzies, and she decided she would just tell the people not to give away any more Warm Fuzzies. She told them that they would run out of Warm Fuzzies if they gave them away. She also gave each person a bag full of Cold Pricklies, and said it would be a good idea to give them to everyone they met. The people believed her. They hid their bags of Warm Fuzzies so no one would get any and they began to give away Cold Pricklies.

Soon all the people in the village were also growling, and were grumpy and sad. Everyone, that is, except the bad witch. She was very happy because finally, all the people were the way she wanted them to be — always growling, grumpy and sad. Even the children hit each other and the dogs would growl and bite each other. The village was not a very nice place.

After many years, a very nice man came to the village. He smiled at people and said friendly things, but no matter what he did, the people would just growl, grumble, and look sad. The man just kept giving away Warm Fuzzies and being nice, and one day a little boy smiled back at him. When the boy smiled he felt so good about smiling, that he wanted to smile all the time. The little boy ran home as fast as he could to look for his bag of Warm Fuzzies that he had put away so long ago. At first he couldn't find them. He looked everywhere, under the bed, in the chest drawers, and in the closet. It had been so long since he saw them that he forgot where he had put them. Finally, he found his bag of Warm Fuzzies at the bottom of his toy box.

The little boy started to give his Warm Fuzzies away. At first the other people grumbled, growled, and looked sad. Then one by one, they tried smiling back at the boy. When they smiled, they found it felt so good that they would go home to find their own bags of Warm Fuzzies. Pretty soon everyone in the village was giving away Warm Fuzzies, and the whole village began to smile, say nice things, and do kind things for each other. Everyone, that is, except for the bad witch. She was so upset when she saw everyone was happy that she moved away, and no one has seen her since.

To this day, that village is a very nice place to be. Everyone smiles, they say nice things, and they do nice things for each other. Maybe if we give enough Warm Fuzzies away, we would make our world a nicer place to be too.

Evaluation of Theme Plans

I like to evaluate the theme plan as the children participate in theme related large group activities, learning centre activities, and during a time allotted to individual children, or during large group discussions following centre time.

Informal observations of each child, and talking with each individual child (when interest in an activity will not be distracted) are useful techniques when assessing each child's level of participation and interest in the theme activities. Through these techniques we can learn a lot about each child's development and interests. We may also gain valuable information which can be used to extend an activity, for removing unused materials from an activity, or for planning new activities. See Figure 3-7 for some of the things I keep in mind as I observe, interview, and conference with the children.

My Suggestions For Teachers

1. The interest and enthusiasm displayed toward activities

2. The interest and enthusiasm displayed toward materials

3. The interest and enthusiasm exhibited toward the theme topic

4. Centres which are most popular or were not chosen at all

5. Discussions between children which are theme related or which discuss any aspects of the topic

6. Comments made by each child who share their ideas following centre time, which give me clues about the suitability of the activity, materials, or theme topic

Figure 3-7

Choosing Themes

Theme plans may be developed on almost any topic and careful consideration should be given to themes chosen for developing a program for young children. First consideration when planning a program should be given to the personal needs of each young child. What we know about child development, learning patterns, and interests of young children helps us to set up a program through which children will develop understandings of things they are interested in, rather than presenting them with ideas which result in fragmented learning, if that. Some topics which are most suitable for young children are shapes, colours, animals, and me, and other topics for which children have developed an experiential background, such as winter, etc. It is very important to be highly flexible. I find that theme plans must be tentative for the reasons I have listed in Figure 3-8.

My Suggestions For Teachers

1. Children may not be interested in a particular theme

2. Children may be so motivated by the theme that it could go on for longer than planned

3. A spontaneous interest of the children may initiate a theme not planned for originally

4. An incident in or out of school may trigger the need for a particular theme (e.g., safety and coping with death)

5. Characteristics of a child or children may initiate the inclusion of a theme focussed on developing understandings (e.g., physical handicaps, ethnic, or cultural)

Figure 3-8

Each teacher's long range plans are generally requested by administrators before the teacher has had enough time to get to know the children well. I find it important to make these plans tentative, allowing for flexibility as the children develop, grow, and learn. See Figure 3-9 for some of the ideas that I like to consider as I make tentative theme plans.

My Suggestions For Teachers

1. The major underlying goals (see Chapter Two)

2. The entering characteristics of children into the program (e.g., socio-economic status of the community, range of ages of children, special needs such as physical disabilities, etc.)

3. Activities that have been set before the school year begins (e.g., field trips, resource visits, swimming dates, skating, program dates, etc.)

4. Special days throughout the school year (e.g., Christmas, Valentine's Day, etc.)

5. Seasons of the year and possible weather patterns and how they may affect certain themes at those times

6. Planned school wide activities (e.g., sports days, concerts, hat days, pancake day, etc.)

Figure 3-9

Figure 3-10 shows a list of tentative themes which may be adjusted to suit your particular needs.

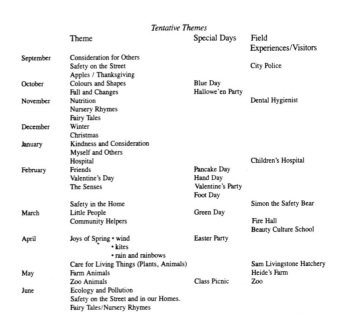

Tentative Themes

	Theme	Special Days	Field Experiences/Visitors
September	Consideration for Others		
	Safety on the Street		City Police
	Apples / Thanksgiving		
October	Colours and Shapes	Blue Day	
	Fall and Changes	Hallowe'en Party	
November	Nutrition		Dental Hygienist
	Nursery Rhymes		
	Fairy Tales		
December	Winter		
	Christmas		
January	Kindness and Consideration		
	Myself and Others		
	Hospital		Children's Hospital
February	Friends	Pancake Day	
	Valentine's Day	Hand Day	
	The Senses	Valentine's Party	
		Foot Day	
	Safety in the Home		Simon the Safety Bear
March	Little People	Green Day	
	Community Helpers		Fire Hall
			Beauty Culture School
April	Joys of Spring • wind	Easter Party	
	• kites		
	• rain and rainbows		
	Care for Living Things (Plants, Animals)		Sam Livingstone Hatchery
May	Farm Animals		Heide's Farm
	Zoo Animals	Class Picnic	Zoo
June	Ecology and Pollution		
	Safety on the Street and in our Homes.		
	Fairy Tales/Nursery Rhymes		

Figure 3-10

Conclusion

Theme planning facilitates an integrated program in which a relationship between learnings is created. Also, through themes the children are more likely to experience the program as a whole, than as a series of unrelated activities. Concepts planned for possible development in one activity can also be developed in other activities.

Daily planning facilitates the organization of theme plans into activities which will occur each day. Chapter Four provides assistance in moving from theme to daily planning.

Daily Plan Day 4 Date Oct 20
9:00 - 9:15
9:15 - 9:30 Arrival, Greeting
9:30 - 9:40 Physical Educ
            Topic: Discussion
9:40 - 9:45 Kindness
            Centres - Introduce

Introduction

The most effective integrated early childhood program in which meaningful learning is most likely to occur is that which is well planned. I find that much attention must be given to the way in which learning situations are structured within each day. Learning should never be left to chance, and each child must have opportunities to learn according to his own individual style and without stress.

As pointed out in Chapter One, an important part of developing a secure, tension free, and relaxed atmosphere in which learning is most likely to occur is to establish routines. These routines may develop more easily if there are fixed times each day when centre time, whole group discussions, physical education, evaluation of centres, and closing activities occur.

Daily planning incorporates theme plans into activities which will occur on a daily basis. These may be large group, small group, and individual activities. In a classroom, where all aspects of learning stem from a theme, the day is regarded as a period made up of divisions of time in which learnings based on the theme are integrated.

Like the theme plan, the daily plan requires a great deal of flexibility. On several occasions, I have found that the children respond to an activity or problem in a much different way than I had anticipated, and it is necessary to adjust plans or to drop an entire theme almost without prior notice.

Teachers vary in ways in which they plan daily instruction. From my own teaching and observations of other teachers, I have evolved a format for planning that suits my particular teaching style. This format is illustrated in Figure 4-1.

Theme Planning to Daily Planning

When careful consideration is given to theme planning (see Chapter Three), the transfer from the theme plan to the daily plan should be relatively easy. This transfer takes place when the broader theme plans are incorporated into activities that will take place on a daily basis. The major objective of a theme is generally very broad and is meant as a statement of an overall objective for the theme plan (e.g., to develop respect for self and others). Related objectives break the major objective into more specific objectives (e.g., to develop an ability to name physical features).

The specificity of the related objectives lends itself more readily to translation into specific concepts and skills which may develop through a particular activity at a centre. Therefore, in daily planning, activities for objectives can more

Daily Plan

Theme   Day   Date

Major objective

9:00-9:15   *Arrival and Greeting; Attendance; Weather/Calendar; Songs/Finger Plays Helpers*
9:15-9:35   *Physical Education*
9:35-9:45   *Discussion Topic:*

Centres   Activity   Skills and Concepts

Housekeeping

Sand

Water

Blocks

Art

Small Train/Construction Toy

Listening

Book

Evaluation of Centres

10:45-11:05   *Music/Creative Drama/Songs and Fingerplays*

11:05-11:20   *Story and Discussion*

Reminders/Notes to go Home

Teacher Aide

Parent Helper

Comments:

(Note: Morning and Afternoon class formats may be copied on different coloured paper)

Figure 4-1

easily be planned if we refer to the related objectives. However, children will not automatically progress toward the objectives set out in the activities. We must present daily activities in ways that will instill a desire to learn and that will motivate children to self discovery and to self chosen involvement in the activity.

The children's concept and skill development is facilitated by the presentation of activities on a daily basis which reflect many different methods of instruction, and by the presentation of a sequence which encourages the 'simple to more complex'.

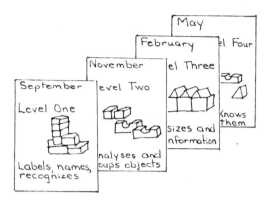

As daily activities are being planned, I find it important to keep the guidelines listed in Figures 4-2 in mind.

My Suggestions For Teachers

1. Activities should be planned so that each experience contributes as much to the total development of each child as possible. I give careful consideration to how the activity may provide for growth in each of the children's areas of development (i.e., social, emotional, physical, intellectual, and creative).

2. Planning should consider special needs of individual children, such as learning styles, different levels of curiosity toward experimenting and manipulating, a need for activity, and a need for a quiet time.

3. Consideration should be given to creating a balance between times of strenuous activities and relaxation, and a balance between times of self expression and group conformity.

4. The activities planned should provide opportunities to ensure the use of a variety of materials over a period of time. If there is too much material out, children may 'window shop'. If there is too little material out, children may compete for the 'bargain table'.

5. Planning should provide backup activities and materials to prevent emergencies that arise because activities are too easy, uninteresting, or too difficult.

6. Planning should take into account the need for variety in the ways content is presented (e.g., films, pictures, speakers, discussions, field trips).

Figure 4-2

A Completed Daily Plan

A sample of a completed daily plan which more clearly demonstrates how a day can be scheduled to focus on varied approaches to teaching and learning is shown in Figure 4-3. This completed daily plan is derived from the theme plan "Kindness and Consideration" (see Chapter Three).

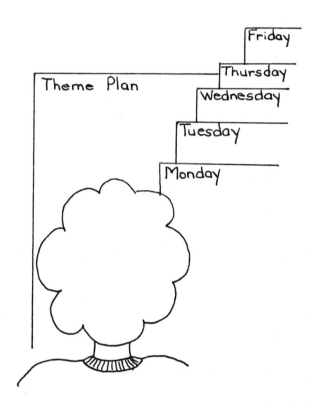

Conclusion

Daily planning assists in structuring the learning environment by incorporating theme plans into activities. Careful planning provides the teacher with confidence about how the day will proceed, so that more emphasis and time can be given to ensuring that meaningful learning is taking place and to ongoing informal evaluation throughout the school day.

The most important part of each day for each child is 'centre time', therefore considerable care and time must be given to planning learning centres. A discussion of learning centres and guidelines which may help in the establishment of learning centres is covered in Chapter Five.

Daily Plan

Theme *Kindness and Consideration*   **Day** *Tuesday*   **Date** *September 17*

Major Objective *To develop an atmosphere of warmth and caring*

9:00-9:15	Arrival and greeting, weather, calendar
	Fingerplay *Two Little Friends*
	Song *If You're Happy and You Know It*
9:15-9:25	Discussion topic *What does it mean to be kind? Encourage children to talk about ways they can be kind to others. Record words on experience chart.*
9:25-9:30	Introduce centres
9:30-10:30	Centre time

Centres	Activity	Skills and Concepts
Home	*Basic Home Centre materials. Include several Teddy Bears.*	*Role playing/dramatization* *Empathy* *Self expression* *Interpersonal skills*
Blocks	*Basic unit blocks (½ unit, single unit, double unit).*	*Sharing* *Attributes of blocks*
Arts/Crafts	*Provide Teddy Bear-shaped art paper, glue, and a variety of materials to make a Teddy Bear collage.*	*Awareness of textures* *Awareness of shapes* *Creative expression* *Vocabulary to describe textures*
Manipulation	*Provide pastel coloured playdough, rolling pins, Teddy Bear cookie cutters, and circle cookie cutters.*	*Creative expression* *Sharing* *Shapes and empty spaces*
Book Centre	*Provide books related to the theme as well as Raggedy Ann and Andy dolls for the children to read with.*	*Interest in books* *Early reading*
Math Centre	*Provide Teddy Bear shapes (ten of each size, five different materials) to sort and classify and to order according to size. Count the number in each group.*	*Classification* *Counting one-to-one* *Ordering sizes* *Awareness of textures* *Awareness of shapes*
Language Arts	*Provide Teddy Bear-shaped books for the children to make their own books using a variety of writing utensils (pencils, felt markers, crayons, chalk).*	*Early writing* *Early reading* *Fine motor* *Sharing* *Expressive*

10:30-10:45	Evaluation of Centres *Ask one child from each centre to talk about what he was doing at that centre.*
10:45-11:05	Creative Movement *Children move like Care Bears around the room (happy, sad, fat, thin). Music "It's a Small World" by Sharon, Lois, and Bram.*
11:05-11:20	Story and Discussion *Just For You by Mercer Mayer*
	Fingerplay/Song *Teddy Bear, Teddy Bear/Magic Penny*

Reminders/Notes To Go Home — *Teddy Bear notices re Teddy Bear day.*

Note to Parent Volunteer — *Please talk with or read to Andy alone for 5-10 minutes today.*

Comments:

Figure 4-3

Introduction

A major part of the day in an early childhood program is given to time for children to be involved in learning centres. During this one and one-half hour period, children pursue activities of their own choice, and may interact in small groups at a particular centre.

A learning centre is a space in the room where the teacher provides a range of planned, sequential experiences that are aimed at helping each of the children develop to their intellectual potential, acquire facility with language, and to develop physically, socially, emotionally, and creatively according to their own unique rate of development.

Learning centres should be structured to stimulate a wide variety of thinking. Media (books, films, materials and tools) should be selected and arranged in an orderly and inviting manner at each centre in the classroom before the children arrive. This prior arrangement of materials and tools at centres helps to focus children's attention and interest on the material placed at each centre. When children are secure in knowing which material is available, they focus more attention on exploring, manipulating, and practicing skills with those materials provided. I find that when I choose and provide material that I judge as appropriate, I can more effectively ensure that each child is continually challenged, not only by the material, but also by the way I present problems to be solved. This prior arrangement of materials seems to give each child the feeling that this is 'especially for me', and then each child seems to take more pride in sharing,

discussing, and cleaning up. Two main points stand out with respect to learning centres. First, learning centres are the basic curriculum in any early childhood program. Second, the key to the successful operation of learning centres lies in the teacher's organization and planning.

Sometimes the children who choose any particular learning centre appear close to the same levels of ability. Most often though, there is a much wider range of abilities between the children involved. The following sections in this chapter will discuss the range of abilities in children and provide some points to consider when planning centres. The role of the teacher and important considerations to take into account when establishing classroom routines will also be covered in this chapter.

Range of Children's Abilities

The diversity in the developing thinking skills of children create a wide range of learning levels within the classroom. All children go through the levels at different rates and the levels attained depend to an extent on the experiences the children have had. Opportunities must be provided at each centre for each child in any particular level. The table in Figure 5-1 is an example of how I have planned for one of the centres to facilitate for needs at four different levels of ability.

Block Centre

Basic Materials Supplied   Unit Blocks

Accessory Materials   Fisher Price People and Animals

Ability Level One	Ability Level Two	Ability Level Three	Ability Level Four
Children acquire basic knowledge about many things, i.e., they label, name, recognize, and follow simple directions.	Children begin to analyze and group objects. First, they discriminate between them and then classify them. This analysis of objects then develops into an ability to make comparisons.	Children begin to organize and use information they have gained through analysis in Level Two. They synthesize acquired information so they can improvise, create, perform, and arrange materials or objects according to their qualities.	Children reach a level of being able to evaluate materials and objects. They can choose, accept, or reject materials and objects on the basis of what they have learned about them.

Evaluating Appropriateness of Materials

Are children involved in labelling or naming the material provided?	Are some children analyzing materials on the basis of similarities and differences?	Are some children using acquired information and knowledge about materials to perform or improvise?	Are some children evaluating materials by choosing, accepting, or rejecting on the basis of what they know about them?

Related Activity

Children just move blocks around, or build simple towers, recognize and name different materials (e.g., blocks, man, woman) and follow simple directions (e.g., handle blocks with care).	Children choose to build with just two different sizes or shapes of blocks, analyze blocks that are the same, different in size and shape, and classify them. Children compare blocks so they can choose the largest, the longest, the smallest, etc., for their purposes in construction.	Children use particular blocks for particular purpose (e.g., longest block for roads), and choose those blocks at a glance. Children give evidence of knowledge about classifications and comparisons and no longer need to place blocks side by side to make comparisons. Children make use of what they already know about the attributes of the blocks as they are constructing, and are able to improvise if what they need is not available. Children are able to arrange materials according to qualities in size, weight, or shape when constructing.	Children show evidence of choosing or rejecting particular blocks on the basis of what they know about them. Children appear aware that some blocks are excellent for one type of structure, while others are more useful for other types (e.g., curved blocks for arches, triangular blocks for peaks of buildings).

Figure 5-1

Planning Learning Centres

When setting up a learning centre, the teacher must look at the abilities, interests, and needs of individual children as well as materials and time available. I find planning activities for learning centres to be an easier task when the points listed in Figure 5-2 are kept in mind.

My Suggestions For Teachers

1. A variety of materials should be provided in a sequential order throughout the school year. Materials should range from simple to complex, and from concrete to abstract as the year progresses.
2. Activities should be provided which develop divergent thinking and creativity (for example, by providing a variety of textured materials, paper, and different sizes of boxes and glue for the children to make their own structures), as well as to develop convergent thinking by having everyone follow a specific example or idea.
3. Time for repetition in different ways should be provided at a centre through the use of diverse media and materials.
4. A selection of diverse media and materials should be provided to allow the children to experiment, to invent, to construct, and to compose, by using the same ideas with different materials.
5. Activities should be provided that will encourage children to think, to explore, and to extend their use of language. For example, after reading *The Very Hungry Caterpillar* (Carle, 1964) and discussing the story pattern, what happened in the story, and the sequence of events in the story, have the children brainstorm ideas for using the same story pattern (e.g., *The Very Happy Teddy Bear,* On Monday he . . . ., On Tuesday he . . . ., etc.). Write the words on sentence strips and place the story in a wall pocket chart as it is dictated by the children.

6. Vocabulary should be introduced and provided that will help the children to express and describe experiences and to relate their findings to background knowledge.
7. Opportunities should be provided for children to record their findings through dictation, through copy writing, or through pictures if and when they desire to do so at each centre. One idea I have used is to provide blank three-page booklets at each centre which have the appropriate centre or topic written on each cover. The children may draw or write in their 'books' at any time during centre time.
8. Materials which arouse aesthetic pleasure and motivate sensory investigation should be provided at each centre and should be set up in an orderly and inviting arrangement that can be easily seen and reached by each child at the centre.
9. A balance should be maintained between noisy and quiet activities, as well as between individual, small group, and large group activities.
10. Display space must be provided so that the children will develop pride in displaying their work at school. Whenever possible, the children's work should be displayed at their eye level.
11. Space at the children's height must be available for temporary storage of equipment used day to day.
12. Simple and easy to follow directions should be established for each centre. When the children begin to show interest in what 'words' say, these directions could be written on cards and posted at or near the centre.

Figure 5-2

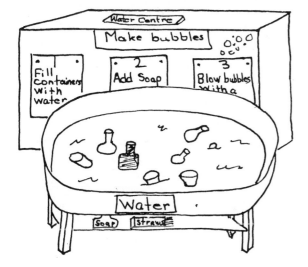

Role of the Teacher

One of the most important roles of the teacher is to provide centres that are attractive, inviting, and conducive to learning so that children will be encouraged to go there.

Besides materials the teacher must provide a positive attitude and express enthusiasm for the activity. Space must be provided in which play can develop, as well as rules for the protection of children and equipment.

The teacher must continuously observe the play in each centre in order to note spontaneous cues that will help to know when to become involved. Manning and Sharp (1977), in their book *Structuring Play In The Early Years At School,* discuss the importance of four different ways in which a teacher could become involved in children's play. These are discussed in the diagram shown in Figure 5-3.

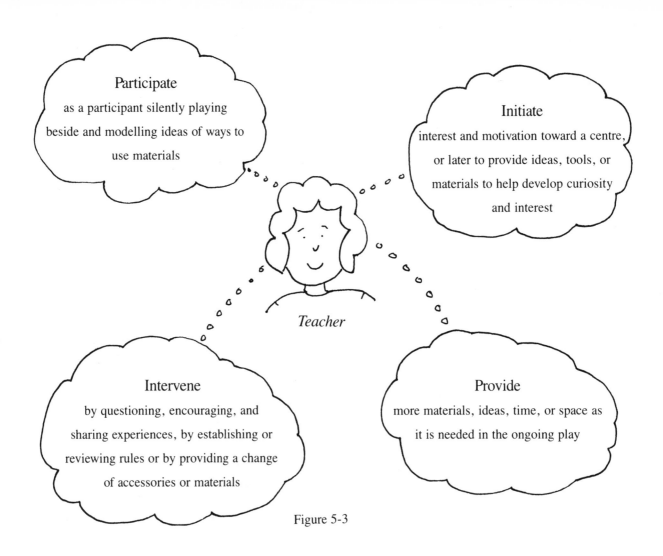

Participate

as a participant silently playing beside and modelling ideas of ways to use materials

Initiate

interest and motivation toward a centre, or later to provide ideas, tools, or materials to help develop curiosity and interest

Teacher

Intervene

by questioning, encouraging, and sharing experiences, by establishing or reviewing rules or by providing a change of accessories or materials

Provide

more materials, ideas, time, or space as it is needed in the ongoing play

Figure 5-3

The teacher's task is to continually assess each centre in terms of its' suitability to each individual child's stage of development, level of learning, learning pattern, and particular needs. This evaluation is essential in order that sequential experiences may be planned which will motivate purposeful learning for each child.

Classroom Routines

Choosing Learning Centres

I find that when I provide structure in the way learning centres are chosen, the children develop a sense of order about their choices. A choosing board (see Figure 5-4) is useful in facilitating and providing underlying structure as the children take turns making a choice about which centre they would like to go to. The time provided for choosing centres should be a relaxed, unhurried part of the day and the

children should feel secure in knowing that the same centres will be offered over a few days. When five to seven centres are provided each week, all based on a particular theme, the children can feel secure in knowing that they can choose one centre today and another tomorrow.

I find the basic rules listed in Figure 5-5 useful in establishing routines and maintaining an underlying structure during centre time.

Maintaining Attractive Learning Centres

Each centre must be attractive, inviting, and conducive to learning. It is necessary that each child who goes to a centre finds space that has been left in a neat and tidy condition. Children must be encouraged to take responsibility in leaving a centre neat and tidy for 'someone else'. Children should learn that they have a role to play in assisting with the development of learning centres by cooperating, by participating and by considering others.

Introducing Learning Centres

I have found that the children feel more comfortable about making centre choices if they are familiar with what is available at each centre. One idea I use is to take the whole group of children to each centre and explain the materials, directions for use, and clean up procedures before talking about centre choices. After this introduction, the children seem more at ease with choosing a centre, probably because they have a better idea of what their choices are. After choices are made, it is very important to accompany small groups of children to 'new centres' to ensure that they understand the directions for the use of materials and routines at that centre. Later, I like to move through all of the centres to discuss materials and directions in small group settings. Individual attention can also be given as you move from centre to centre throughout the entire centre time.

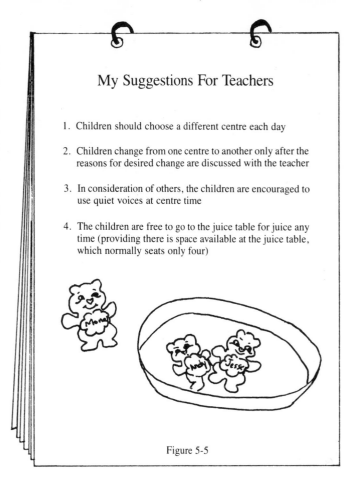

My Suggestions For Teachers

1. Children should choose a different centre each day

2. Children change from one centre to another only after the reasons for desired change are discussed with the teacher

3. In consideration of others, the children are encouraged to use quiet voices at centre time

4. The children are free to go to the juice table for juice any time (providing there is space available at the juice table, which normally seats only four)

Figure 5-5

Assisting Volunteer Adults at Learning Centres

Signs posted at each centre can provide information to volunteer adults about things they can do to be most effective in assisting at each centre. Figure 5-6 shows an example of a volunteer sign at the Home Centre.

Choosing Boards

Use a large sheet of plywood to construct a choosing board. Insert cup hooks (large size) in rows as shown. The Centre cards which indicate the Centre choices are hung along the left side of the board. The children's name tags are hung along the bottom of the board. The hooks to the right of each Centre card indicate how many children may go to each centre. To accommodate for variation in the number of children allowed to go to each centre, I put a different number of blank cards on the hooks on the right side of the board. The blank cards indicate that the hooks cannot be used and help the children to read 'how many' may go to each centre. They can count the number of empty hooks and keep track of the number of spaces remaining as other children are making choices.

Figure 5-4

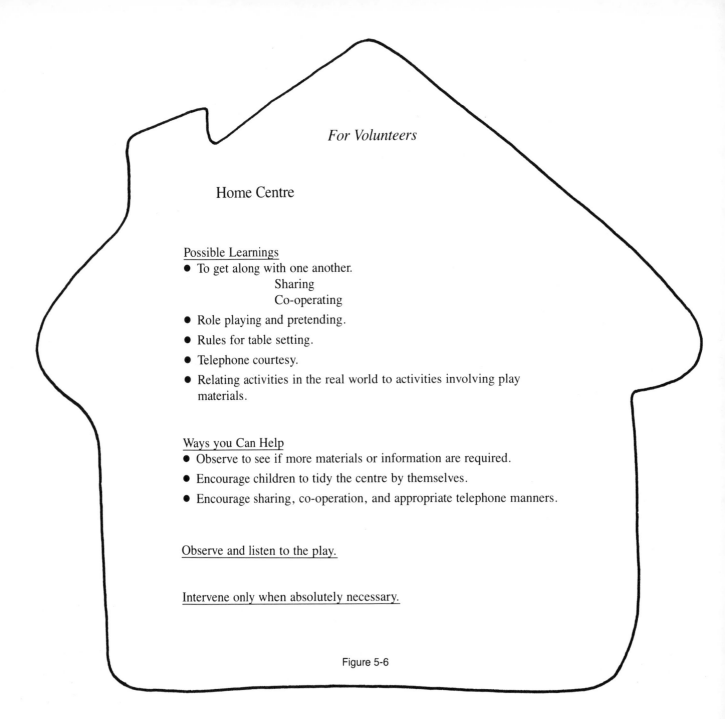

For Volunteers

Home Centre

Possible Learnings
- To get along with one another.
  - Sharing
  - Co-operating
- Role playing and pretending.
- Rules for table setting.
- Telephone courtesy.
- Relating activities in the real world to activities involving play materials.

Ways you Can Help
- Observe to see if more materials or information are required.
- Encourage children to tidy the centre by themselves.
- Encourage sharing, co-operation, and appropriate telephone manners.

Observe and listen to the play.

Intervene only when absolutely necessary.

Figure 5-6

Conclusion

Planning for learning centres takes up most of the early childhood teacher's planning time. Also, most of the children's time in school is taken up by involvement in learning centres. Learning centres must consist of sequential experiences which are planned to provide for the development and growth of each child.

The appropriateness of the learning centre and other activities in an early childhood program, the effectiveness with which they are presented, and the efficiency with which they are assessed are major considerations. Equally important is the way in which assessments are recorded so that they provide meaningful information for the teacher to refer to later.

Record keeping should be both efficient and accurate to be of use in the teacher's ongoing planning, and as a subject of parent and public concern. Chapter Six will provide ideas for assessing the early childhood program and for keeping records.

6

Introduction

The trend in teaching has become more informal, individualized, and small group centred. This affects how we do assessments and the kind of records we keep. Also, the increased need for political accountability, and the current transient nature of our population emphasize the need for teachers to keep appropriate and accurate records of children's educational progress.

Traditional checklists of specific skills are no longer adequate as forms of record keeping in early childhood programs which follow the more informal philosophy of teaching through themes. What we need in this more informal approach is to keep records of both the children's participation in activities and the quality of their performance at the activity.

It seems that most teachers experience similar temporal and technical problems with record keeping. I have not found a complete solution to these problems, but have found the points that I have listed in Figure 6-1 to be helpful to me as far as time commitment and the development of formats is concerned.

This chapter provides an overview of several forms of record keeping that have worked for me. This overview should not be perceived as the 'only way' but may provide a

basis on which to develop or re-evaluate your record keeping system.

For organizational purposes, record keeping will be discussed under the headings *Theme Planning, Daily Planning,* and *Learning Centres. Long Range Planning* will not be included as it is generally broad and vague, and leaves little opportunity to be used for assessment and recording of children's attainments. A section on record keeping for reporting and parent interview purposes will also be included in this chapter.

Theme Planning

This section will discuss the two major sources of information useful for keeping records during ongoing theme plans. These are the outline of themes to be covered during the school term, and the four levels of children's learning.

Outline of Themes

This is an outline of tentative themes to be covered in the early childhood program from September to June. This

My Suggestions For Teachers

Design

All records should have

- a clear, simple layout
- clear printing
- the child's name in a prominent place
- clear section headings
- sufficient space for comments
- a prominently placed key to explain use of colour coding, abbreviations, or symbols

Content

The content of a record should be

- directly related to the purpose of the record
- brief, simple, and contain only relevant information

Figure 6-1

outline has evolved from long range plans and is often requested by the administration early in the school year. An example of one tentative theme outline which I found useful may be seen in Figure 3-10. As the year progresses this outline gives me an idea of what I have already covered in the program.

The outline of themes must be 'tentative' especially if you do not know the children's needs. As you get to know the children, you may notice physical handicaps or developmental delays, or you may find some topics to be too difficult or not challenging enough for some of the children.

Levels of Learning

Recorded information on the observed level of learning of each child provides an idea of the range of abilities in the class. This is excellent supplementary information which can be used when planning or developing materials. Figure 6-2 shows a sample assessment and recording sheet and how I use it to assess and record levels of learning.

Daily Planning

This section covers those records kept on a daily basis. These are anecdotal records and interviews with individual children.

Levels of Learning

Name of child _____

Level		Date Assessed	Comments
One	Acquires basic knowledge about many things		
	Labels		
	Gives simple directions		
Two	Analyses and groups objects		
	Discriminates between Objects.		
	Classifies objects		
Three	Organizes and uses information gained in levels one and two		
	Places objects in order of quality of intensity (colour, sound, size, etc.)		
Four	Evaluates materials and objects		
	Accepts or rejects certain materials.		
	Expresses reason for choosing certain materials and objects		

Figure 6-2

Anecdotal Records

Anecdotal records are recordings of unusual or irregular behaviours of a child, and are usually written on individual cards or on pages of a notebook, each card or page assigned to a different child. The recording must be dated, and should state exactly what occurred in a nonjudgmental way. Only observable behaviour should be noted, and if observer inferences are made, it should be noted that they are inferences (see Figures 6-3).

Interviews with Individual Children

Interviews with children can provide insight into their likes, dislikes, learning style, and social behaviour. We can also assess children's language by listening for sentence length, complexity of language used and for clarity of speech and grammar as they converse naturally during an informal interview. We can also probe children's language when they retell familiar stories, or describe incidents in their lives.

Interviews help to fill in gaps about things we cannot see when we just observe. Often, a different side of children is seen when we interview them.

Interviews should be informal and relaxed, and can cover a variety of topics, but it is best to focus on one topic for each interview, and to keep the interview short. Some examples have been referred to earlier in this book. These were 'What is it about your classroom that makes you feel good?', and 'What makes you sad?'. Other topics may focus on the current theme, friends, recess activities, a particular activity, or a particular centre.

Learning Centres

This section will discuss activity records, play behaviour and interests, summary records of skills, and folder collections of materials.

Activity Record

A record of activities of each child's involvement at learning centres is valuable, particularly when children are choosing different centres to go to. The activity record may be filled in by the individual child (see Figure 6-4), or may be filled in by the teacher (see Figure 6-5). In both cases, I like to have the records easily accessible so they can be used to keep track of the activities each child has been involved in, or to record when children have completed a particular activity or task.

When the children are filling out their own activity records, they can put one diagonal line through the picture when beginning the task, and complete the cross with another diagonal line when the activity is completed (see Figure 6-4).

When I am filling out the activity record, I like to make a diagonal line for beginning the task, another for completion (making a cross). I also find it helpful to mark a dot beside names of particular children who will not be doing that activity (see Figure 6-5) because it is too easy, too difficult, or maybe it has been necessary to divert a child's attention to another activity.

Anecdotal Record

Child's name _____ Jane Smith _____

Date of birth _____ August 12, 1979 _____

Date	Observed behavior	Comments/Inferences
Oct 12/84	Jane cried when her mother left. She was very quiet all day.	Jane is having a difficult time adjusting to short separations from her mother

Figure 6-3

43

Name _____			
Week beginning _____			
Home	Blocks	Sand	Water
Painting	Arts and Crafts	Listening	Pocket Chart

Figure 6-4

Play Behaviour and Interests

Insight into children's play behaviour and interests can be gained through observing them while they play. Information about space needed for play, time it takes play to develop, use of equipment and materials, and rules followed or developed by the children can also be gained through observing children at play. This kind of information is valuable in further planning or for assessing objectives set for the centre being observed. A format I have adapted from others for recording this information can be seen in Figure 6-6. This format provides space for the name of centre, kind of play, date, time of observation, and comments.

Summary Record of Skills

The summary record of skills is a checklist of skills which the child has acquired to date (see Figure 6-7). This information is useful to refer to when writing reports, at parent/teacher interviews, and when transferring student information. I like to do this record four times a year, prior to each reporting period. Colour coding may be used to check skills achieved during the respective reporting period.

Collection of Materials

I like to prepare an individual file folder for each child, and collect the following materials to be stored in it (if the material is date stamped before storing, it can be used more effectively to show children's progress, when writing reports and at parent/teacher conferences):

General materials For example, children's artwork or writing.

Specific materials For example once a month, I like to ask each child to draw a picture of herself and write her name on the page.

Note At the end of the year, the total collection may be put into booklets using a 'head' silhouette of the child as a design for the cover, and given to someone as a gift for a special occasion (e.g., Father's Day).

44

Week of _____

	Sand	Water	Blocks	Art/Crafts	Home Centre	Mathematics		Language Art		Manipulation	Listening	Book	Painting						

Figure 6-5

Observing Learning Through Play

Centre _____ Kind of Play _____ Date _____ Time _____

Names of children involved	
Amount of space used for play (Is the whole centre area required, or does play occur in a section of the area?)	
Time children concentrated. (Note the longest and shortest time)	
Equipment and materials used most	
Equipment and materials not used	
Materials used to improvise other things	
Rules made by the children while they played	
Classroom or centre rules broken or adapted by the children to suit their play needs	

Figure 6-6

Summary Record of Skills

November ____ February ____ April ____ June ____

Name _____ ☐ Birthday _____ ☐ Age _____ ☐ (at September 1)

Address _____ ☐ Telephone Number _____ ☐

Handedness _____

Colours	Red	Blue	Yellow	Green	Orange	Purple	Brown	

Shapes

Sequences ideas when	describing own experiences
	retelling stories

Recognizes rhyming words

Recognizes letters	a	b	c	d	e	f	g	h	i	j	k	l	m	n	o	p	q	r	s	t	u	v	w	x	y	z
	A	B	C	D	E	F	G	H	I	J	K	L	M	N	O	P	Q	R	S	T	U	V	W	X	Y	Z

Sight words	he	was	to	and	is	the	in	of	I	a	it	that

Recognizes numerals	1	2	3	4	5	6	7	8	9	10	11	12	13	14	15	16	17	18	19	20	
Counts one-to-one	1	2	3	4	5	6	7	8	9	10	11	12	13	14	15	16	17	18	19	20	
Rote counts to	1	2	3	4	5	6	7	8	9	10	11	12	13	14	15	16	17	18	19	20	

Patterning	Copies patterns	Makes own patterns	

Days of the week	Sunday	Monday	Tuesday	Wednesday	Thursday	Friday	Saturday

Months	January	February	March	April	May	June	July	August	September
	October	November	December						

Ties own shoes	Dresses self	Does up zippers, buttons, etc.	

Recognizes	Left	Right

Knows own name	First	Middle	Last	

Recognizes own name in print	First	Middle	Last	

Writes own name	First	Middle	Last	

Knows own birthday _____

telephone number _____

address _____

Comments:

Reporting and Parent/Teacher Interviews

Reporting

The primary purpose of any reporting system is to communicate an assessment, and the reports we write in school are an assessment of an individual child's progress.

When the report is written for the parents, we must be sensitive to the parents' feelings. Parents are often emotionally involved with their children, and because of the way the report is written they may feel the teacher is passing judgement on their role as parents. I like to take considerable care when making written comments. Some comments like the following are empty and meaningless, and convey little, if any information about the child's progress:

    I enjoy having Mona in my class.

    It is a pleasure to teach Janet.

    Andy enjoys Physical Education.

    Jesse has trouble in Mathematics.

A comparison between good and poor reporting may be seen in Figure 6-8.

Reports may be written in anecdotal form, in the form of a checklist, or in a pictorial format. I have found the most desirable to be a combination of pictorial, which the children can read (see Figure 6-9), and the anecdotal report (see Figure 6-10). When children can interpret their own reports, they become more interested in their own progress and may develop a sense of pride in their own accomplishments.

Good Reporting	Poor Reporting
Social Adjustment:	Social Adjustment:
John displays a happy attitude toward school activities, and accepts classroom rules and routines. We are encouraging John to interact with others more during centre time.	John enjoys school and knows the rules and routines. He engages mainly in parallel play, but is getting better at associative play.
Possible parent reactions to this report:	Possible parent reactions to this report:
• satisfaction with comment about John being happy as it does not make assumptions. • draws particular attention to John's need to interact with others.	• makes assumptions about John's feelings • vague — what do rules and routines refer to? • what is parallel play? • what is associative play? • what does 'getting better at' mean?

Figure 6-8

I know my telephone number.

I know the colours.

I enjoy listening to stories.

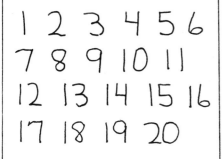

I can count to ___.

I can tie my shoes.

Mary Louise Day
John Charles Man

I know my full name.

Figure 6-9

Anecdotal Report

Social Development

_____

_____

Emotional Development

_____

_____

Physical Development

_____

_____

Cognitive Development

_____

_____

Figure 6-10

The parent/teacher interviews are very important, and the teacher must be well prepared for them. I find it very helpful to jot down things to discuss during the interview while I am writing reports. It is also helpful to keep brief notes of the decisions made between the parent and myself during interviews.

Again, it is important to keep in mind, the emotional attachment of the parents toward the child, that parents may not feel at ease during the interviews, and that they need time to talk.

Interviews can be very draining for the teacher, both emotionally and intellectually. I have found the suggestions (see Figure 6-11) useful for making interviews more pleasant for both the parents and myself.

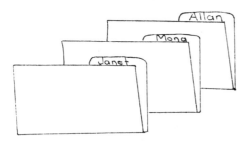

My Suggestions For Teachers

1. Be well prepared and well organized. Have the files organized in the same order as the interviews will occur.

2. Sit on the same side of the table as the parents. This arrangement will help everyone to feel more at ease during the interview.

3. Be positive in all comments.

4. Tell parents briefly what the objectives of your program have been, and what the child has achieved.

5. Set parents at ease by smiling, making an informal comment, and by having samples of the child's work available.

6. Encourage the parents to express their points of view.

7. Let the parents know you are writing brief points about the interview (questions, concerns, etc.).

8. Have some materials ready in case parents ask how they may help their child at home. Examples are lists of titles of wordless picture books, titles of predictable books, and titles of children's literature of good quality.

9. If it appears that more time is required, arrange another interview with the parents. Do not keep others waiting.

10. Allow yourself at least one or two minutes between interviews, not to catch up on notes, but to relax.

Figure 6-11

Conclusion

The informal nature of present day early childhood programs indicates a need for a different type of record keeping than the more skills oriented formal programs.

I find that theme outlines and awareness of children's levels of learning are useful information when planning the early childhood program. Information recorded daily, such as anecdotal records and interviews with particular children is useful for planning a program which suits the individual needs of the children.

Records about children's participation at centres and the play behaviour and interests of children provide useful information for planning centre activities.

One of the purposes of keeping records and of collecting children's material is to provide information which is useful when writing reports, or during parent/teacher interviews. Reports and interviews must communicate an assessment which is accurate and which is also sensitive to the feelings of parents. Teachers must be very discriminating when choosing records or information to record which will provide helpful information to use both in program planning and when conveying assessment information.

Bibliography

Allen, P. *Mr. Archimedes Bath*. London: The Bodley Head Ltd., 1980.

Carle, E. *The Very Hungry Caterpillar*. Toronto: Scholastic Book Services, 1964.

Cherry, C. *Please Don't Sit On The Kids*. Belmont, California: Fearon Pitman Publishers, Inc., 1983.

Clift, P., Weiner, G., Wilson, E. *Record Keeping In Primary Schools*. London: MacMillan Education, 1982.

Manning, K., Sharp, A. *Structuring Play In The Early Years At School*. London: Ward Lock Educational, 1977.

Mason, E. *A Tale From The Care Bears, A Sister For Sam*. Parker Brothers, 1983.

Maxim, G. W. *The Very Young*. Belmont, California: Wadsworth Publishing Co., 1980.

Parry, M. *From Two To Five*. London: MacMillan Education Ltd., 1976.

Yardley, A. *Learning To Adjust*. London: Evans Brothers Ltd., 1973.

Yardley, A. *Senses and Sensitivity*. London: Evans Brothers Ltd., 1970.

Yardley, A. *The Teacher of Young Children*. London: Evans Brothers Ltd., 1974.

Yardley, A. *Young Children Thinking*. London: Evans Brothers Ltd., 1974.

Wells, G. *Learning Through Interaction*. Cambridge: Cambridge University Press, 1981.

This theme covers a two-week period.

Major Objectives

To develop concepts of colours.

To develop concepts of shapes.

Related Objectives

To develop familiarity with 'colour' words.

To develop familiarity with primary colours.

To develop an awareness of the results when mixing primary colours.

To match, classify, and order colours and colour intensities.

To develop an awareness of different shapes.

To develop an idea about making patterns from shapes.

To develop familiarity with 'shape' words.

Motivation

Read a book like *Brown Bear, Brown Bear* (Martin, 1967). Discuss the colours in the story and in the classroom.

Read a book like *The Missing Piece* (Silverstein, 1976). Discuss the shapes in the story and in the classroom.

Large Group Activities

Introduce the following poem in a wall pocket chart (see Resource Materials for pictures), using appropriately coloured markers to write 'colour' words:

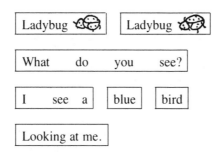

Have extra blank cards available to substitute for the 'colour' words in the poem:

e.g., | yellow | | red |

Build onto this poem by encouraging the children to suggest other colours and things through brainstorming, e.g., orange, green, cat, chair, etc.

For movement activities, use the following Hap Palmer records:

    "Parade of Colours"

    "Colours"

    "Triangle, Circle, or Square"

See Resource Materials for filmstrips and a film that could be shown and books that could be read to the children.

Discussion Topics

- Discuss the primary colours red, yellow, and blue, and examine how often they appear in the environment.
- Demonstrate and discuss mixing the colours red, yellow, and blue.
- Discuss the colours 'we' are wearing today.
- Discuss basic shapes (e.g., a circle, triangle, square, rectangle) in our classroom environment.
- Discuss shapes of designs and patterns on clothing, shoes, etc.

Centre Activities

Home Centre
Week One
Using plastic eyedroppers, have children put drops of primary food colouring, which have been diluted in water in baby food jars, onto white tissues placed in play plates, bowls, cups, and trays. The jars containing the coloured water should be labelled with appropriately coloured words.

Week Two
Home Centre closed.

Sand Centre
Week One
Provide a set of sand bags in three different shades of blue and three different sizes. Have children fill and then order these bags according to size, colour or weight.

Week Two
Introduce two more sets of bags:
• three shades of red in three different sizes
• three shades of yellow in three different sizes
Have children classify the bags into sets, and then fill and order them according to size or colour and compare weights.

Block Centre
Week One
Present a variety of coloured blocks (four or five different colours) and sheets of construction paper in matching colours. Have children build with red blocks on red construction paper, blue on blue, etc.

Week Two
Present 'long' sheets of paper with outlines of different shaped blocks drawn on them. Have children match blocks to appropriate outlines.

Language Arts Centre
Week One
Provide eight houses made of different coloured construction paper and a variety of small coloured objects (e.g., party favours) to be sorted onto the colour houses. The 'colour' words on the colour houses should be written in a colour that matches the 'colour' word.

Week Two
Introduce words and pictures for a chart activity which follow the same story pattern as *Brown Bear, Brown Bear* by Bill Martin. The 'colour' words and pictures may vary, for example:

Also provide pictures of shapes which may be used in place of the animal pictures and used together with the 'colour' words, for example:

Concepts/Skills Which May be Developed

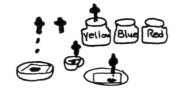

Primary colours
Mixing primary colours to make secondary colours
Association of 'colour' words with appropriate colour

Ordering largest to smallest
Ordering smallest to largest
Ordering intensity of colour
Properties of dry sand
Comparing and ordering weight

Ordering largest to smallest
Ordering smallest to largest
Ordering intensity of colour
Properties of dry sand
Matching weights
Comparing weights

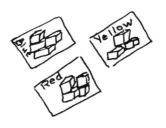

Classifying colours
Matching colours
Creative expression

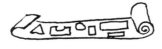

Awareness of shape outline of blocks
Matching shapes
Patterning

Associating 'colour' words with colours
Classification
Counting

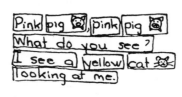

Story patterns
Sentence patterns
Left to right progression
'Colour' words
Early reading

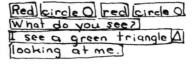

Shape recognition
Shape vocabulary

52

Arts and Crafts Centre
Week One
Provide large sheets of construction paper cut into shapes (e.g., a circle, square, triangle, rectangle). These sheets should also be in a variety of colours. Provide cloth and paper scraps of different textures and different colours for the children to glue onto appropriately matching sheets to make a collage.

Week Two
Provide small red, blue, and yellow paper shapes and large shapes cut from plain white paper (e.g., a circle, square, triangle, rectangle). Have children make border patterns around the edge of the large white paper shapes.

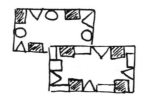

Water Centre
Week One
Change the colour of the water each day and provide the appropriate label for the colour of the water. Then provide about five different-sized funnels and pouring containers such as plastic cups. Have children experiment with pouring.

Week Two
Provide clear water in the water table and as the children begin playing in the water, add drops of two different colours of food colours (e.g., red and blue, red and yellow, yellow and blue, etc.). Provide word labels written in appropriately matching colours for the colours introduced. (The same containers may be used from Week One for pouring.)

Paint Centre
Week One
Introduce finger painting by applying the three primary colours to each child's choice of large paper cut into either a square, circle, triangle, or rectangle.

Week Two
Introduce painting at the easel. Provide paper cut into various shapes and paint in the three primary colours. Have children choose their own shape on which to paint a picture.

Mathematics Centre
Week One
Introduce a 'shape' and 'colour' Bingo game in which each of the four shapes (i.e., circle, triangle, rectangle, square) are presented in a variety of colours on the playing card. A set of small cards which includes a variety of combinations of colours and shapes is available for the 'caller'. The caller shuffles the cards and calls each one in turn. The player looks over his playing card for the 'shape and colour' called, and places a 'chip' on those that are on his card.

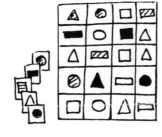

Concepts/Skills Which May Be Developed

Shape awareness
Matching colours
Naming shapes
Creative expression

Shape recognition
Patterning
Creative expression

Colour awareness
Shape awareness
Conservation of water
Controlling flow of water

Colour awareness
Mixing colours
Conservation of water
Associating 'colour' words
   with appropriate colour

Sensory exploration
Primary colours
Secondary colours
Shapes
Creative expression

Primary colours
Secondary colours
Shapes
Creative expression

Shape awareness
Colour awareness

Centre Activities

Week Two

Provide parquetry shapes and pattern cards.
Have children match parquetry shapes onto
those appearing on the pattern card.

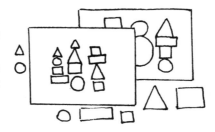

Awareness of space and shapes
Patterning

Also provide sets of colour samples to arrange in
order of intensity (these may be obtained from
paint shops).

Colour intensity
Ordering
Primary colours
Secondary colours

Culminating Activity

A 'colour' day may be planned in which the children will wear the colour selected for that day (e.g., Blue Day, Yellow
Day, etc.). On that day, activities may mainly involve colour objects appropriate to that 'colour' day.

Resource Materials

Filmstrips

The Blue Balloon, 6 minutes, by Coronet.
The Orange Pumpkin, 6 minutes by Coronet.
The Green Caterpillar, 6 minutes by Coronet.
The Purple Flower, 6 minutes by Coronet.
The Red Car, 6 minutes by Coronet.
The Yellow Bird, 6 minutes by Coronet.

Films

Colour, Colour Everywhere, 14 minutes, by Coronet.

Records

Palmer, Hap, 'Parade of Colours', *Learning Basic Skills Through Music,* Volume 2.
Palmer, Hap, 'Colours', *Learning Basic Skills Through Music,* Volume 1.
Palmer, Hap, 'Triangle, Circle, or Square', *Learning Basic Skills Through Music,* Volume 2.

Books

Anglund, John Walsh. *What Colour Is Love?* New York: Harcourt, Brace and World, Inc.
Carle, Eric. *My Very First Book of Colours.* New York: Crowell, 1974.
Hutchins, Pat. *Changes, Changes.* New York: Collier Jr. Paperbacks, 1973.
Macdonald Starters: Science, No. 14. *Rainbow Colours.* London: Macdonald and Company Ltd., 1974.
Martin, Bill. *Brown Bear, Brown Bear.* New York: Holt, Rinehart and Winston, 1967.
O'Neill, Mary. *Hailstones and Halibut Bones.* New York: Doubleday and Company, Inc., 1961.
Rachlin, Sidney, S. Ditchburn, B. Bannon and Sawicki, E. *First Steps to Mathematics.* Calgary: Braun and Braun Educational
    Enterprises Ltd., 1984.
Silverstein, Shel. *The Missing Piece.* New York: Harper & Row Publishers, Inc., 1976.
Silverstein, Shel. *The Missing Piece Meets the Big O.* New York: Harper and Row Publishers, Inc., 1981.
Tison, Annette. *Adventures of Three Colours.* Columbus: C. E. Merrill Publ. Co., 1980.
Wolff, Robert Jay. *Feeling Blue.* New York: Charles Scribner's Sons, 1968.
Wolff, Robert Jay. *Seeing Red.* New York: Charles Scribner's Sons, 1968.

Pictures

This theme covers a two-week period.

Major Objectives

To develop an ability to analyse something as common as apples.

To provide opportunities for learning and development through relating a familiar topic to each centre.

Related Objectives

To develop an awareness of the attributes and characteristics of apples.

To develop sensory awareness through tasting, smelling, touching, and looking at apples.

To learn where apples come from.

Motivation

Tell the following story about the shape of the star in the apple:

> Once upon a time there was a little girl who was tired of all her toys. She asked her mother for something to do, and her mother told her she could go outside and "look for a little red house that is round and shiny, has no windows and no doors, but has a star inside".

> The little girl looked and looked. Finally she asked the dog if he could help. The girl and the dog both looked but could not find the house with the star inside. (They go through the same routine after they meet a cat, a horse, a cow and a chicken.)

> Then the little girl, the dog, the cat, the horse, the cow, and the chicken meet a lady and ask her if she has seen a little red shiny round house with a star inside. The lady asked them to come with her and she took them to an apple tree. There, with her knife, she cut an apple in half horizontally. There was the star!

Following this story, cut a round red shiny apple in half horizontally. Discuss the star shape, the seeds, and the shape of the half apple.

Large Group Activities

Introduce the following action verse, suiting actions to words:

Two Red Apples

Away up high in the apple tree (reach arms up)
Two red apples smiled at me (smile).
I shook that tree as hard as I could (shake tree).
Down came the apples (hands motion to ground)
And m-m-m they were good (rub tummy)!

Show and discuss different apples such as Granny Smith, Golden Delicious, and MacIntosh. Introduce the following poem in a pocket chart, using appropriately coloured markers to write the 'colour' words, and to colour the 'apple' picture clues in each word card:

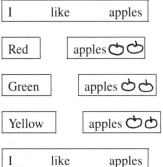

Encourage the children to move the words around on the chart as they match the 'colour' word with the appropriate 'apple' word card.

Provide several Granny Smith, Golden Delicious, and MacIntosh apples and a graph. Have children place the apples in appropriate sections on the graph.

green	🍎							
yellow	🍎	🍎						
red	🍎	🍎						

Then count the apples placed on the graph. Compare the apples to see which there are most of, least of or the same.

See Resource Materials for a film that could be shown and books that could be read to the children.

55

Discussion Topics

- Discuss apple colours, shapes and sizes.
- Cut an apple into wedges for smelling and tasting. Encourage the children to brainstorm words to describe the smells and tastes. Record the words on an experience chart under the appropriate heading of smell or taste.
- Discuss what kinds of things people can do with apples (i.e., eat them, cook them, make pies, bob for them, etc.).

Centre Activities

Home Centre
Week One
Present Granny Smith, Golden Delicious, Mac-Intosh apples in various sizes, and balance scales for comparing weights.

Week Two
Introduce green, yellow, and red blocks. Have children classify apples and blocks and compare weights of red apples with weights of red blocks, green apples with green blocks, and yellow apples with yellow blocks.

Language Arts Centre
Week One
Provide apple-shaped booklets with unlined paper for the children to draw apples and write the 'colour' words red, yellow, and green as well as the word 'apple'. The children may also wish to copy the following 'apple' story from the pocket chart:

I	like	apples
Red		apples
Green		apples
Yellow		apples
I	like	apples

Week Two
Provide individual desk pocket charts and the following word cards:

I	like	apples
Red		apples
Green		apples
Yellow		apples
I	like	apples

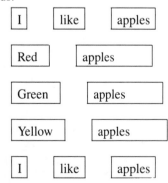

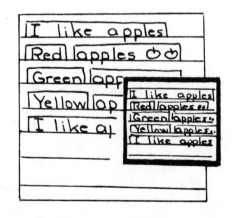

Have children match the words in their desk pocket charts to those in the large wall pocket chart.

Concepts/Skills Which May be Developed

Awareness of different kinds of apples
Vocabulary
Comparing sizes and colours
Comparing weights

Classification
Matching colours
Comparing weights

Self expression
Control of writing utensils
Handwriting
Creative expression
Word and letter recognition

Matching words
Word recognition
Awareness of what a word is

Arts and Crafts Centre

Week One

Soak sponge with red, yellow, or green paint and set in styrofoam tray. Cut apples in half horizontally and press apple-half onto the sponge. Then stamp apple on apple-shaped paper. Encourage the children to look for the 'star' shape. Also use other objects to make prints (e.g., sponge, block, fork, fabric).

Week Two

Make apple collages on apple-shaped paper. Provide different textured paper and fabric in red, yellow, and green for the children to use in their collage. Encourage the children to dictate words to describe their collage.

Sand Centre

Week One

Provide five different sizes of red cloth apple-shaped sand bags for the children to fill, order, and compare (see Resource Materials for instructions).

Week Two

Introduce two more red cloth apple-shaped sand bags, of which one is bigger than the largest introduced in Week One, and one is smaller than the smallest. The children may fill, order, and compare the sizes and weights of these bags.

Water Centre

Week One

Provide a variety of clear plastic bottles, funnels and pouring containers (e.g., tumblers, small bottles). Colour the water in the water table red and have children experiment with pouring.

Week Two

Colour the water green and provide the same materials as in Week One. Put masking tape on the outside of the clear containers to be used as markers. Have children fill each container to the level indicated by the masking tape.

Mathematics Centre

Week One

Provide sets of five sizes of red construction paper apples, and five sizes of yellow construction paper apples. Have children place these in order of size or classify them according to colour or size. (These paper apples will last much longer if they are laminated.)

Week Two

Provide three sets of ten picture cards, one set of red apples, one set of yellow apples, and another set of green apples, each set ranging from one to ten. Have children order each set from one to ten or match cards with the same number of apples.

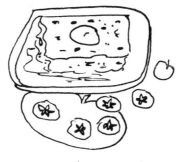

Concepts/Skills Which May Be Developed

Colour awareness
Patterning
Shape awareness

Colour awareness
Shape awareness
Awareness of textures
Creative expression
Verbal expression

Ordering largest to smallest
Ordering smallest to largest
Comparing weights
Ordering weights
Properties of dry sand

Ordering largest to smallest
Ordering smallest to largest
Comparing weights
Ordering weights
Properties of dry sand

Conservation
Measuring in non-standard units
Controlling the flow of water

Measuring in non-standard units
Controlling the flow of water
Conservation

Ordering sizes
Matching sizes
Classifying
Comparing

Counting
One-to-one correspondence
Ordering
Classifying
Comparing

Manipulation Centre
Week One

Provide red playdough made from the following recipe:

  500 mL flour
  125 mL salt
   30 mL cooking oil

Put food colouring into warm water and add gradually to the above until the desired consistency is reached.

Cut apple shapes from cardboard for the children to use as patterns for tracing and cutting apple shapes out of the dough.

Week Two

Manipulation Centre closed.

Concepts/Skills Which May Be Developed

Fine motor development
Creative expression
Conservation
Negative shapes
Form and shape

Culminating Activity

Discuss making applesauce, and then write the following recipe for making applesauce on the experience chart:

To make applesauce

  We need apples.
  We will peel the apples.
  We will cut the apples into pieces.
  We will put the pieces in a pan.
  We will add water and sugar.
  We will cook the apple pieces, water, and sugar together.
  We will cook the applesauce.
  We will eat the applesauce.

Another recipe is available in *First Steps to Mathematics* (Rachlin, et al, 1984).

Send a note home with the children, asking each child to bring an apple to school. Make applesauce as a large group activity. Parent volunteers may assist by cutting apples in half or quarters for the children during this activity. The children can then peel the apple pieces and cut them in small pieces. Have adults walk around the room to collect the apple pieces. Cook apple pieces in an electrical dutch oven in the room and add water and sugar as desired during cooking.

Resource Materials
Filmstrips

How apples grow, National Apple Institute, Washington, D.C.

Books

Aliki. *The Story Of Johnny Appleseed.* Englewood Cliffs, N.J.: Prentice Hall, 1963.
Curry, Nancy. *An Apple Is Red.* Glendale, California: Bowman Publishing Corp., 1967.
Hagrogian, Nonny. *Apples.* New York: Macmillan, 1972.
LeSieg, Theo. *Ten Apples Up On Top.* New York: Random House, Inc., 1961.
Mayer, Mercer. *Just For You.* New York: Golden Press, 1975.
Rachlin, S. L., Ditchburn, S. J., Bannon, B., and Sawicki, E. *First Steps To Mathematics.* Calgary, Alberta: Braun and Braun Educational Enterprises Ltd., 1984.

Patterns

Instructions for apple-shaped sand bags.

Follow the directions used for the Teddy Bear-shaped sand bags (see Theme "Kindness and Consideration" in Chapter 3), except, instead of cutting out the Teddy Bear shapes, cut different sized circles from red coloured fabric.

This theme covers a two-week period.

Major Objectives

To develop a greater awareness and understanding of nursery rhymes.

To help each child draw on background knowledge to make sense of new ideas.

Related Objectives

To develop familiarity with rhythm in language.

To develop an awareness of rhyming words.

To develop a familiarity with patterns in language.

Motivation

Show the nursery rhyme film *All In The Morning Early* (Bosustow, 1969). Present several nursery rhyme books and identify some nursery rhymes shown in the film. Involve the children in saying some of the nursery rhymes together.

Large Group Activities

Identify nursery rhyme characters in illustrations in different nursery rhyme books. Show how they are the same and how they are different.

Brainstorm and record actions of characters in nursery rhymes in wall pocket chart sentence strips.

For example:

| The mouse ran up the clock. |

| The cow jumped over the moon. |

| Old Mother Hubbard went to the cupboard. |

| Jack and Jill went up the hill. |

Have word cards available that match words in the sentence strips.

For example:

| clock | | Jill | | moon | | hill |

Have children match the word card to the appropriate word on the sentence strip.

Brainstorm and record characteristics of one nursery rhyme character at a time on experience chart paper.

For example: Mary Mary Quite Contrary
pretty
kind
nice to everyone
cheerful

Listen for rhyming words as a nursery rhyme is recited in the large group.

Record nursery rhymes on wall pocket chart strips and have children recite them together.

See Resource Materials for a film that could be shown and books that could be read to the children.

Discussion Topics

- Encourage the children to talk about the reality and the fantasy about things that happen in nursery rhymes such as 'Humpty Dumpty', 'Jack and Jill', 'Old Mother Hubbard', and 'Hey Diddle Diddle'.
- Discuss what different nursery rhyme characters look like, what they wear, and what they do.
- Ask for volunteers to tell which nursery rhyme character they would like to be. Ask why they would like to be that character and what they would do.

Centre Activities

Sand Centre
Week One

Post nursery rhyme pictures near the Sand Centre and have a nursery rhyme book available. Introduce the sand wheel and have children role play nursery rhyme characters with objects such as wooden people, sheep, dogs, pigs, dishes, spoons, cows, and cats.

Week Two

Draw Humpty Dumpty features on L'Eggs panti-hose containers and place on a wall made of blocks. Also post the words of the rhyme 'Humpty Dumpty' and have children illustrate and write or copy words about Humpty Dumpty into unlined egg-shaped booklets.

Mathematics Centre
Week One

Provide two sets of ten number cards, one set with number symbols from one to ten, the other with one to ten pictures of nursery rhyme characters or objects (see Resources Materials). The children can sort, order, classify, or match these cards.

Week Two

Provide sets of nursery rhyme character pictures. One set has one picture, the others have five, four, three and two identical pictures. Introduce a graph format on which the children may record the appropriate number of each character.

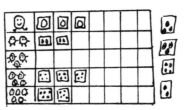

Language Arts Centre
Week One

Have children manipulate nursery rhyme characters on a flannel board while retelling nursery rhymes. Then have children draw or write in unlined booklets of various shapes (see Resource Materials for patterns) such as pumpkins, pigs, castles, crowns or watering cans.

Week Two

Introduce sentence strips with the words for the nursery rhyme 'Humpty Dumpty' in the wall pocket chart. Provide an extra set of sentence strips for the children to match to those in the pocket chart. Later provide a set of word cards for the children to match to those in the pocket chart.

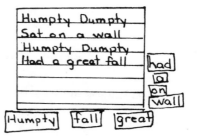

Concepts/Skills Which May be Developed

Properties of dry sand
Role playing
Sequencing ideas
Nursery rhymes

Properties of dry sand
Role playing
Sequencing ideas
Nursery rhymes
Early writing

Number recognition
Counting
Ordering numbers
Classification
Comparing
Matching

Graphing
Counting
Comparing

Sequencing ideas
Early reading
Early writing
Expression of ideas
Role playing

Early reading
Matching sentences
Matching words
Word recognition
Sequencing ideas

Water Centre

Week One

Introduce small watering cans, spray bottles, and clothes sprinklers. Have children explore how these work.

Week Two

Provide small watering cans, spray bottles as in Week One, and containers for the children to pour, spray, and sprinkle water into.

Block Centre

Week One

Post pictures of nursery rhymes and provide wooden people, animals, small blocks, and plain paper so the children may draw what they are planning to build with blocks for nursery rhyme characters.

Week Two

Make pattern cards (see samples in Resource Materials) for the attribute blocks in the shape of castles. Have children match the blocks to the castle design.

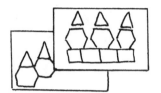

Arts and Crafts Centre

Week One

Provide construction paper body shape figures (see Resource Materials for pattern) and scrap materials such as yarn, fabric, lace and tissue paper. Have children dress the figures like nursery rhyme characters. Label and display completed characters on a 'nursery rhyme' bulletin board.

Week Two

Provide a variety of scraps of construction paper, fabric, yarn, and tissue paper for the children to make houses, trees, walls, etc., to complete the 'nursery rhyme' bulletin board display set up in Week One.

Concepts/Skills Which May Be Developed

Properties of water flowing in different ways

Properties of water flowing in different ways
Controlling the flow of water

Planning
Role playing
Early writing
Creative expression

Space and shapes
Classifying
Comparing
Outline of shapes

Creative expression
Fine motor development
'Nursery rhyme' vocabulary

Creative expression
Fine motor development
'Nursery rhyme' vocabulary

Culminating Activity

Remove all of the materials displayed on the 'nursery rhyme' bulletin board, and sort them according to nursery rhymes. Have children work in small groups and paste each set on a separate page. The pages can be laminated and made into a nursery rhyme book with a cover that has been designed by the children.

Resource Materials

Films

All In The Morning Early, 10 minutes, by Stephen Bosustow, 1969.

Books

Alderson, Brian. *Cakes And Custard: Children's Rhymes.* London: Heinemann, 1974.

Lobel, Arnold. *Gregory Griggs And Other Nursery Rhyme People.* New York: Greenwillow Books, 1978.

Mongomerie, Norah. *This Little Pig Went to Market.* London: Bodley Head, 1966.

Mother Goose. *Gray Goose And Gander And Other Mother Goose Rhymes.* New York: Thomas Y. Crowell, 1980.

Ness, Evaline. *Old Mother Hubbard And Her Dog.* New York: Holt, Rinehard and Winston, 1972.

Opie, Iona. *Oxford Nursery Rhyme Book.* London: Oxford University Press, 1955.

Sendak, Maurice. *Hector Protector And As I Went Over The Water.* New York: Harper and Row, 1965.

Stobbs, William. *House That Jack Built.* Oxford: Oxford University Press, 1983.

Williams, Sarah. *Round and Round The Garden.* Oxford: Oxford University Press, 1983.

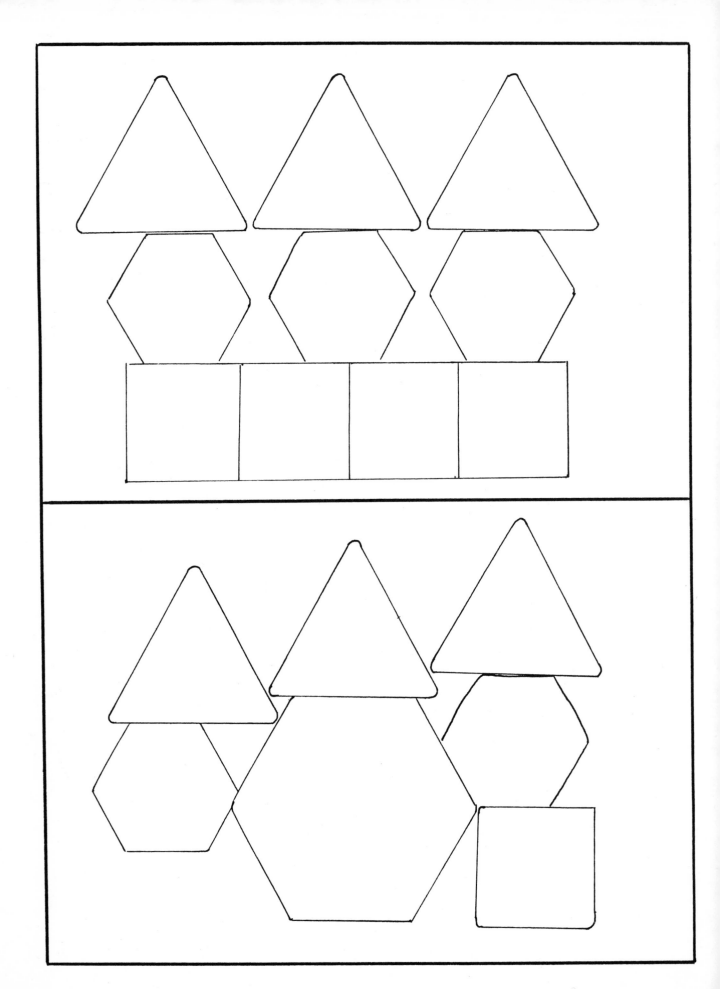

This theme covers a one-week period.

Major Objectives

To develop an awareness of changing seasons.

To develop an understanding of the event called Hallowe'en.

Related Objectives

To develop an understanding of what happens to trees in the fall.

To develop an awareness of shapes and colours of leaves.

To develop an awareness of Hallowe'en symbols such as pumpkins, Jack-o-lanterns, ghosts, witches, and cats.

To develop an understanding of the importance of safety at Hallowe'en.

Motivation

Take a walk in the neighborhood to gather leaves. The leaves may be pressed by placing them in magazines.

Read *Witches* (Rawson and Cartwright, 1979). Discuss the different kinds of witches talked about in this book.

Large Group Activities

Visit the nearest grocery store to buy a pumpkin. If possible, arrange a trip to see a pumpkin growing in a garden.

Carve a pumpkin and provide opportunities for each child to taste, feel, smell, and touch the seeds and pulp from the pumpkin. Discuss the different sensory experiences.

Go on a nature walk to collect leaves, seeds, dried grass, and weeds to make a fall collage for the bulletin board.

Introduce (using appropriately coloured markers to write 'colour' words) the following poem in the wall pocket chart:

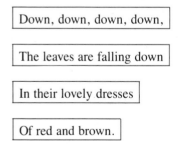

Provide individual word cards for the children to match to those in the pocket chart. For example:

Place other 'colour' word cards (e.g., yellow or green) over the words 'red' and 'brown', then say the poem again.

See Resource Materials for a film that could be shown and books that could be read to the children.

Discussion Topics

- Discuss fall and fall changes.
- Discuss Hallowe'en events such as dressing in costumes, trick or treating, etc.
- Discuss safety at Hallowe'en.
- Discuss the fantasy of witches, ghosts, monsters, and black cats.
- Discuss how to make a jack-o'-lantern both prior to and after carving one.

Centre Activities

Concepts/Skills Which May be Devloped

Home Centre
Week One
Introduce masks, skirts, capes, wigs and hats for role playing.

Role playing
Vocabulary
Self expression

Language Arts Centre
Week One
Introduce the following poem in the pocket chart:

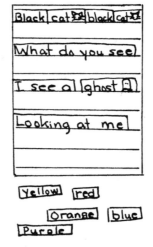

| Black | cat | black | cat |

| What do you see? |

| I see a ghost |

| Looking at me. |

Provide extra 'colour' word cards written with appropriately coloured markers, and word cards with picture clues. For example:

| witch | bat |
| dog | jack-o'-lantern |

The children may exchange the 'colour' and word cards to develop different poems.

Early reading
Vocabulary
Sentence pattern
Creativity

Arts and Crafts Centre
Week One
Provide triangle-shaped pieces of black paper. Have children fold two of the corners over to form the ears of a cat. Add other cat face features and the body and legs by gluing on yarn, fabric, or scraps of paper.

Shape recognition
Fine motor coordination
Creative expression

Paint Centre
Week One
Provide orange, green, yellow, and red paint and sponges held by clothespins to paint leaves onto a tree-shaped (see Resource Materials for pattern) paper.

Creative expression
Fine motor coordination
Colour recognition

Mathematics Centre
Week One

Provide two sets of ten paper jack-o'-lanterns (see Resource Materials for patterns) with each jack-o'-lantern in the set having a different number of teeth, ranging from one to ten. Have children order the jack-o'-lanterns from one to ten by counting the teeth. They may also arrange the jack-o'-lanterns into pairs.

Sand Centre
Week One

Introduce miniature toy people, toy vehicles, twigs, stones, dried grass, weeds, acorns, and leaves. Have children build roads, hills, fields and fences, to be used for role playing with the toy people and vehicles.

Concepts/Skills Which May Be Developed

Counting
Ordering
Comparing
Matching

Role playing
Planning
Cooperation
Fall as a season

Culminating Activity

Plan a Hallowe'en party with the children. Discuss decorations, food, drink, and costumes. Make paper pumpkin placemats and decorate styrofoam cups with orange pumpkins and black cats. Show a film such as *Hallowe'en Safety,* or go on a parade through the school to show other classes the children's costumes or invite the principal to come in to read a Hallowe'en story.

Resource Materials
Films

Hallowe'en Safety, 11 minutes, Producer Centron Films, 1977.

Books

Bridwell, Norman. *Clifford's Hallowe'en*. New York, N.Y.: Tour Winds Press, 1966.
Foster, Doris Van Lieu. *Tell Me, Mr. Owl*. New York, N.Y.: Lothrop, 1957.
Fachenback, Dick. *Ida Fanfanny*. New York, N.Y.: Harper and Row, 1978.
Hurd, Edith. *So So Cat*. New York, N.Y.: Harper and Row, 1964.
Jasner, Walter. *Which Is The Witch?* New York, N.Y.: Pantheon, 1979.
Keats, Ezra Jack. *Trip*. New York, N.Y.: Greenwillow Books, 1978.
Rawson, Christopher and Cartwright, Stephen. *Witches*. Tulsa, Oklahoma: Hayes Books, 1980.

This theme covers a two-week period.

Major Objectives

To provide an understanding of fairy tales.

To help each child draw on background knowledge to help make sense of new ideas.

Related Objectives

To develop each child's ability to predict and confirm or reject predictions.

To develop each child's ability to sequence events.

To develop an awareness of fairy tale story patterns.

Motivation

Show a fairy tale film (see Resource Materials for suggestions). Turn off the sound and show it again. Discuss the events and what the characters are saying in the film.

Display fairy tale books and fairy tale pictures wherever possible around the room.

Large Group Activities

Read and discuss different versions of the same fairy tale.

Encourage the children to dramatize fairy tale events as others observe.

Show fairy tale films, then turn off the sound and ask children to tell the story as the film is re-run.

Sing the following song:

Repeat with the following words:

She lived in a big castle,
Big castle, big castle.
She lived in a big castle
Big castle.

A wicked fairy cast a spell.
Fair Rosa slept for hundred years.
A handsome prince came riding by.
He woke fair Rosa from her sleep.
They lived for many a happy year.

See Resource Materials for films that could be shown and books that could be read to the children.

Discussion Topics

- Discuss the sequence of events in familiar fairy tales.
- Discuss good, evil, charming, beautiful, and wicked characters in relation to particular fairy tale characters (e.g., charming prince).
- Encourage the children to make up and dictate 'Once upon a time' stories. Record these stories on experience charts and read them together.
- Tape record children's versions of fairy tales, listen to, and discuss them.

Centre Activities

Sand Centre
Week One
Dampen the sand in the sand table and provide containers for the children to mold the sand so they can build castles.

Week Two
Make sand castle pictures as follows: Have children draw a castle on paper, spread glue on it, sprinkle sand onto the glue and shake off the excess sand. Materials such as tin foil for windows, cardboard for doors, and toothpicks for trim should also be available for the children to glue onto their castle pictures.

Shapes and space
Conservation
Properties of damp sand
Creativity

Creative expression
Manipulation
Properties of sand
Properties of glue

Arts and Crafts Centre
Week One
Make a fairy tale mural to be hung in the hallway. Have the children construct fairy tale characters from paper plates, and construction paper, using yarn or cotton batting for hair, and fabric for clothing, etc. Encourage the children to dictate a story about their character. The story should be posted near the appropriate character.

Creativity
Self expression
Early writing
Oral expression

Week Two
Provide empty boxes (cereal boxes, etc.), scissors, paint, and felt markers for the children to construct castles. The castles may be displayed on a shelf or by attaching them to the mural created in Week One. Stories dictated about the castles should be displayed near each appropriate castle.

Creativity
Self expression
Early writing
Oral expression

Manipulation Centre
Week One
Provide playdough (see ''Valentine Theme'' for recipe), rolling pins, plastic knives, and a garlic press (for making hair or clothing) for the children to make fairy tale characters. The playdough characters may be baked at 100°C (250°F) for one hour, and then painted the following day.

Fine motor development
Self expression
Creativity
Shapes and space

Week Two
Introduce fairy tale puzzles and continue with the playdough activity.

Classifying
Comparing

Water Centre
Week One
Place various sized containers in the water table. Fill each with a little water, Ivory dish soap, and about five mL of glycerine. Then have children blow bubbles with disposable plastic straws. Also place a sign in the centre indicating that this is a 'Bubble' Centre.

Concept of bubbles
Rainbow colours in bubbles
Blowing through a straw
Early reading

Week Two
Continue the 'Bubble' Centre and have children draw or write about bubbles in unlined circle-shaped booklets.

Early writing
Self expression

Block Centre

Week One

Provide paper and felt markers for children to make plans of what they want to construct. Encourage castle building by posting castle pictures.

Week Two

Provide castle-shaped paper (see Resource Materials for a pattern) for the children to draw plans of what they want to build. Also provide castle-shaped booklets for the children to draw and write about completed constructions.

Carpentry Centre

Week One

Introduce scraps of wood and styrofoam for the children to glue together to construct fairy tale castles.

Week Two

Continue building fairy tale castles. Provide tempera paint for the children to paint their structures. Also provide blank booklets in which the children may illustrate or write about their structures.

Language Arts Centre

Week One

Read the rebus story "The Little Red Hen" (Clark, 1983) with the children. Discuss the sequence of events. Provide sentence strips for the pocket chart as well as pictures which may be switched around to create different sentences or stories as follows:

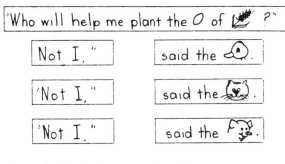

Also provide duplicate word cards which the children may match to words that are the same.

Week Two

Make sentence strips of the sentences used in Week One for the desk pocket charts. Include blank cards so the children may illustrate their own pictures to be used at the end of each sentence. Also provide blank booklets in which the children may draw and write their own stories.

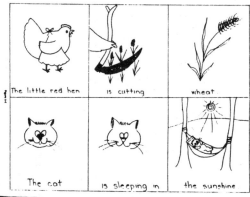

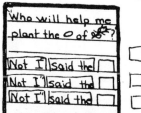

Concepts/Skills Which May Be Developed

Planning
Expressing ideas on paper
Following through with plans
Gross and fine motor skills
Early writing

Planning
Expressing ideas on paper
Following through with plans
Gross and fine motor skills
Early writing

Creativity
Self expression
Fine motor development
Shapes and space

Creativity
Self expression
Fine motor development
Shapes and space
Early writing

Early reading
Listening
Sequencing ideas
Story patterns
Sentence patterns

Early reading
Listening
Sequencing ideas
Story patterns
Early writing

Home Centre

Week One

Display fairy tale books and pictures, then introduce the following materials for the role playing of fairy tales: decorated construction paper crowns, tiarras, gaudy jewelry, sequined clothes, filmy gowns, wigs, ragged clothes, etc.

Week Two

Continue with materials and books as in Week One.

Concepts/Skills Which May Be Developed

Role playing
Vocabulary
Sequencing events
Self expression

Culminating Activity

Parents could be invited to the school to look at the fairy tale bulletin board display. The fairy tale display may also be presented to the local library or community centre for display.

Resource Materials

Films

Elves and the Shoemaker, 30 minutes, by Allan David Productions, 1967.
Little Red Riding Hood, 10 minutes, Ray Harryhausen, 1951.
Rumpelstiltskin, 12 minutes, by Perspective Films, 1981.
Shoemaker and the Elves, 14 minutes, by Gakken Film Company, 1961.

Books

Clark, Karen. *Language Experiences With Children's Stories.* Calgary, Alberta: Braun and Braun Educational Enterprises Ltd., 1983.
De Regniers, Beatrice. *Red Riding Hood.* New York: Atheneum, 1972.
Galdone, Paul. *Cinderella.* New York: McGraw-Hill, 1978.
Grimm, Jacob. *Bremen Town Musicians.* New York: Charles-Scribner's Sons, 1968.
Perrault, Charles. *The Three Wishes.* Mahwak, N.J.: Troll Associates, 1979.
Rawson, Christopher and Cartright, Stephen. *Princes and Princesses.* Tulsa, Oklahoma: Hayes Books, 1980.

Patterns

This theme covers a two-week period.

Major Objectives

To develop an understanding of the season called winter.

To develop each child's ability to help make sense of new ideas by drawing on past and present experiences.

Related Objectives

To develop basic understandings of the physical properties of snow, ice, frost, and icicles.

To develop concepts of winter weather.

To develop ideas for appropriate dress for winter weather.

Motivation

If possible bring snow and ice into the classroom to examine and discuss.

If snow has fallen very recently, go for a walk over undisturbed snow. Listen to sounds that can be made in the snow and look at tracks made in it.

Read *The Snowy Day* (Keats, 1962). Discuss what happens throughout the story.

Large Group Activities

Go for a walk in newly-fallen snow across a park or school yard. Make tracks in the snow that are close together, far apart, in curved pathways, in straight pathways, and that zig zag.

If it is snowing, look through a magnifying glass at snowflakes on sleeves or at snowflakes on dark velvet cloth.

Introduce the following sentence patterns and pictures (see Resource Materials for chart-sized pictures) in the wall pocket chart:

There	is	snow	on	the	🚌
There	is	snow	on	the	🚗
There	is	snow	on	the	⛄
There	is	snow	on	the	🧤
There	is	snow	on	the	🌲

Change the noun by substituting other 'winter' words for the word "snow" in each sentence.

For example:

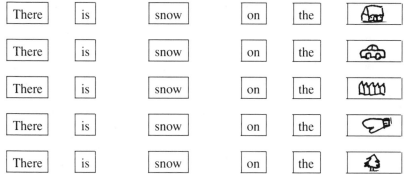

Snow	There	is	snow	on	the	🚌
Frost	There	is	frost	on	the	🌷
Ice	There	is	ice	on	the	👟

Say the following action rhymes, suiting actions to rhymes:

Mitten Weather

Thumb in the thumb place,
Fingers all together,
This is the song we sing
In mitten weather.

Doesn't matter whether
They're made of wool or leather.
Thumb in the thumb place,
Fingers all together,
This is the song we sing
In mitten weather.

Walking In The Snow

Let's go walking in the snow,
Walking, walking, or tiptoe.
Lift your one foot way up high,
Then the other to keep it dry.
All around the yard we skip,
Watch your step, or you might slip.

See Resource Materials for films that could be shown and books that could be read to the children.

Discussion Topics

- Discuss what snow is, what snow is made of, what snow can do, where snow comes from, what can be made out of snow, how snow feels, tastes, looks, sounds, and smells, and what shapes can be seen in snowflakes.
- Discuss what frost is.
- Discuss what ice is.
- Discuss what the weather is like in the winter and how we take care of ourselves in this kind of weather.
- Discuss the clothing we wear in winter and the texture of fabrics in coats, scarves, mittens, hats, etc.

Centre Activities

Concepts/Skills Which May be Developed

Mathematics Centre

Week One

Provide a pan of snow, various-sized containers, and a balance scale. Have children compare weights of snow balls or of various-sized containers filled with snow.

Properties of snow
Measurement
Shape awareness
Ordering

Week Two

Freeze water in containers of different sizes and shapes. Then introduce them to the water table. Have children compare the weights of the different shapes of ice.

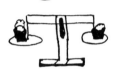

Concept of freezing
Change from water to ice
Measurement
Shape awareness

Block Centre

Week One

Provide large sheets of paper and writing utensils and have children draw plans of what they want to build with large white sheets or squares of styrofoam.

Planning
Creative expression
Cooperation
Sharing

Week Two

Provide 20 cm by 20 cm squares of styrofoam and four one-metre square sheets of paper. Have children make predictions and then cover the surface area of the paper with the styrofoam squares to determine how many 20 cm squares of styrofoam are required to cover the one-metre square sheet of paper.

Planning
Creative expression
Predicting
Counting
Measurement
Surface area

Language Arts Centre

Week One

Put the following sentence strips and pictures in the wall pocket chart:

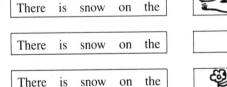

Early reading
Sentence patterns
Matching words

Have children move the pictures around to make different sentences.

Week Two

Using the same sentence strips as in Week One, leave one sentence complete and cut the others into word cards. Have children arrange the word cards to make the complete sentence, and also move the pictures between sentences. By comparing word cards the children may determine how many are the same.

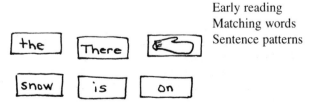

Early reading
Matching words
Sentence patterns

Sand Centre
Week One
Provide snow and different-sized containers to be used for molding and shaping snow. Odd mittens collected from the lost and found box may be used during this activity and later returned to the lost and found box.
Week Two
Same as Week One.

Arts and Crafts Centre
Week One
Provide coarse yarn and long sheets of paper. Cut the sheets of paper into 5 cm strips lengthwise to about 10 cm from each end. Then have children weave paper scarves with the yarn and paper.
Week Two
Provide mitten-shaped (see Resource Materials for pattern) paper. Have children decorate pairs of mitten shapes, gluing on bits of trim and scrap materials.

Paint Centre
Week One
Introduce fluffy soap for fingerpainting. The fluffy soap can be made by beating 250 mL of Ivory soap flakes together with 125 mL water. Have children fingerpaint on dark-coloured paper.
Week Two
Provide sheets of paper on which paper mittens have been glued. Have children paint a person on the sheet whose hands are in the mittens.

Home Centre
Week One
Provide materials such as mittens, scarves, boots, hats, fur, snowsuits and a sled to encourage 'winter' role playing and use of 'winter' vocabulary.
Week Two
Introduce different-sized dolls and matching winter clothing such as sweaters, warm jackets, hats, and snowsuits. Have children dress dolls in appropriate clothing.

Water Centre
Week One
Provide non-standard unit containers for the children to fill with ice cubes or snow to a line indicated by masking tape. Encourage the children to watch the levels of ice or snow in their containers while the ice or snow melts.
Week Two
Add ice cubes and snow to the water in the water table as in Week One. Provide empty cans in which holes have been punched along the side, as well as along the bottom. Encourage the children to discuss why the water flows out while the ice does not.

Concepts/Skills Which May Be Developed

Properties of snow
'Winter' vocabulary
Creative expression

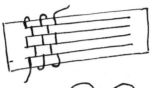

Fine motor development
Creative expression
Colour awareness
Patterning

Creative expression
Matching
Surface area
Patterning

Creative expression
Tactile sensations
Vocabulary

Creative expression
Manipulation

Role playing
'Winter' vocabulary

Role playing
'Winter' vocabulary
Matching
Ordering

Properties of ice
Change in matter
Measurement

Properties of ice and snow
Water pressure
Measurement

75

Culminating Activity

Organize a variety of outdoor activities such as making angel patterns in the snow, stepping into paint powder and making tracks, comparing different patterns of footprints, and building snow castles. Follow these activities by serving hot chocolate with marshmallow snowmen.

Resource Materials

Films

Ladybug, Ladybug, Winter is Coming! 10 minutes, Coronet, 1976.
Look Around You In Winter, 17 minutes, Murl Deusing Film Production, 1978.
Winter Comes To The Forest, 11 minutes, Coronet, 1964.

Books

Bartoli, Jennifer. *Snow On Bear's Nose.* Chicago: A. Whitman, 1976.
Bunting, Anne. *Winter's Coming.* New York, N.Y.: Harcourt, Brace Jovanovich, 1977.
Keats, Ezra Jack. *The Snowy Day.* New York: Viking Press, 1962.

Patterns

This theme covers a one-week period.

Major Objectives

To develop an appreciation for traditional Christmas activities.

To develop kindness and empathy toward others.

Related Objectives

To develop an awareness of Christmas symbols such as trees, stars, wreaths, holly, angels, stockings, ornaments, reindeer, Santa Claus, and elves.

To realize that Christmas is a time to share and to give gifts to others.

Motivation

Motivation for a Christmas theme will happen easily during the Christmas season through commercials on television and displays in shopping malls. The children will develop a more meaningful understanding of Christmas through listening to stories and through discussions about Christmas Day.

Large Group Activities

Dramatize being elves in Santa's workshop. Have children build their favorite toy.

Do creative movement by being Santa Claus, the reindeer, or elves.

Take a walk through a shopping mall to look at decorations and lights. After this excursion, brainstorm and record Christmas words.

See Resource Materials for books that could be read to the children.

Discussion Topics

- Discuss the kinds of toys that are advertised on television. Many of the children will probably have had experiences with toys that break easily or do not work well.
- Discuss and record things that may be happening in Santa's workshops.
- Discuss what Santa, his elves, and his reindeer do at Christmas.
- Discuss and record the children's ideas about Christmas.

Centre Activities

Home Centre
Week One

Introduce a small artificial Christmas tree, ornaments, boxes, wrapping paper, tape, and ribbon. Have children decorate the tree and wrap presents. Then provide popcorn, cranberries, and threaded needles for the children to make food garlands to hang on trees outside for the birds.

Block Centre
Week One

Provide brightly coloured stockings. Encourage children to draw plans for fireplaces, to build them, hang the stockings on them, and write about them in fireplace-shaped booklets (see Resource Materials for pattern).

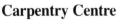

Carpentry Centre
Week One

Have children make Christmas gifts from scraps of styrofoam, wood, fabric, and glue. After completed, they may paint them and wrap them up for someone. Also encourage the children to write or dictate and then copy descriptions of their creations.

Concepts/Skills Which May be Developed

Role playing
Creative expression
Vocabulary
Sharing
Fine motor development

Planning
Early writing
Role Playing
Attributes of blocks

Creative expression
Colours and textures
Shapes
Manipulative
Measuring

Arts and Crafts Centre
Week One

Provide pre-cut arms, legs, mitts, boots, and a hat for each of the children to glue onto a paper plate to create a Santa Claus. Then have each of the children cut eyes, a nose, and a mouth for their Santas from scraps of blue and red paper. Cotton batting should also be provided for Santa's beard, hair, and eyebrows

Language Arts Centre
Week One

Encourage the children to write or dictate and copy a letter to Santa. These letters may be dropped into the mailbox after a copy has been xeroxed for a bulletin board display.

Cooking Centre
Week One

Make Christmas cookies with the children, using a sugar cookie recipe (see "Valentines and Friends" Theme for recipe). While the cookies are baking have children illustrate or write about what they did. When the cookies are baked and cooled, provide icing and a variety of decorations for the children to decorate the cookies to give to someone.

Concepts/Skills Which May Be Developed

Creative expression
Vocabulary
Manipulation

Early writing
Self expression
Early reading

Sensory
Creative expression
Change in matter
Patterning
Shapes and space

Culminating Activity

Concert evenings for parents or carol singing at senior citizens' homes together with displays are excellent culminating activities. Sharing food and donating unused toys to less fortunate people helps to develop empathy, sharing, and kindness.

Resource Materials
Books

DePaola, Tommie, *The Legend of Old Befana*. New York: Harcourt, Brace Jovanovich, 1980.
Frost, Frances. *Christmas In The Woods*. New York: Harper and Row Publishers, 1942.
Livingston, Myra Cohn. *Christmas Poems*. New York: Holiday House, 1984.
Spier, Peter. *Peter Spier's Christmas!* Garden City, New York: Doubleday, 1983.
Stevenson, James. *The Night After Christmas*. Toronto, Ontario: Scholastic Book Services, 1981.
Wiberg, Harold. *Christmas at the Tomten's Farm*. New York: Coward-McCann, Inc., 1970.

Patterns

This theme covers a two-week period.

Major Objectives

To develop consideration for others.

To develop appreciation and respect for others.

Related Objectives

To develop cooperative behavior.

To develop a desire to share materials.

To develop respect for rules and routines.

Motivation

Read *Two Good Friends* (Delton, 1974). Discuss Bear and Duck's friendship and how they could help each other.

See Resource Materials for other books that could be read.

Large Group Activities

Say the following action verses, suiting actions to words:

We Can Jump

We can jump, jump, jump.
We can hop, hop, hop.
We can clap, clap, clap.
We can stop, stop, stop.
We can nod our heads for 'yes'.
We can shake our heads for 'no'.
We can bend our knees a little bit,
And sit down slow.

Who Feels Happy?

Who feels happy, who feels gay?
All who do, clap their hands this way.
Who feels happy, who feels gay?
All who do, nod their heads this way.
Who feels happy, who feels gay?
All who do, tap their shoulders this way.

Encourage the children to dictate things they would do to be kind to each other. Record their ideas on an experience chart.

Encourage the children to dictate ways in which they could help to make new children feel welcome.

Have the children move around the room in creative ways (e.g., high, low, slowly, quickly, sadly, and happily) alone, then with one partner and finally with two partners.

Introduce the poem "Big and Little" (Rachlin, et. al., 1984).

Big and Little

Everything
That you see
In the world
Has to be
Big or Little.
Which am I?

I'm little next to
Sea or sky
But big next to a
Bee or fly,
Big or Little
Which am I?

Next to
A house
I'm small.
Next to
A mouse
I'm tall.
Big or Little
Which am I?

See Resource Materials for books that could be read to the children.

Discussion topics

- Discuss rules for group discussions, e.g., only one person speaks at a time, take turns talking, and listen while others talk.
- Discuss things that are the same about people, and things that are different.
- Discuss what people wear and whether what they wear makes them a nice person.
- Discuss classroom rules and routines, and why we have them.

Centre Activities

Concepts/Skills Which May be Developed

Language Arts Centre
Week One
Present pictures of clothing and articles which have been cut from catalogues and glued on cardboard. Have each of the children select pictures to represent members in their family.

Matching
Comparing and sorting
Detail awareness

Week Two
Introduce sets of pictures of people, with each pair only differing in some small detail.

Detail awareness
Similarities
Differences
Comparing

Shuffle and mix the cards. Have the children sort the pictures into sets that are identical.

Mathematics Centre
Week One
Introduce safety pins and pieces of cloth to which different numbers have been attached. Have children attach the appropriate number of pins onto each piece of cloth.

Manipulation
Counting
One-to-one relations

Week Two
Introduce a counting "Tug of War" game. See below:

Sharing
Cooperation
Counting
One-to-one relations

This game requires two players, one die which the children take turns using and one marker which is set in the middle of the game board, which the children share as they play. Player One shakes the die and moves the marker towards his end of the game board. Player Two then shakes the die and moves the same marker back towards her end of the game board. The winner is the person who is able to go off his end of the game board first.

Writing Centre
Week One
Introduce prepared booklets on 'myself' with a cover as shown:

Myself
My name is _____
My age is _____

Each inside page should suggest a different idea about 'myself'. Some ideas are:

Things I like to do
Things I do not like to do
Food I like
Food I don't like
People I like

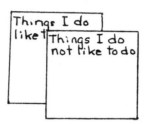

Have children complete books by drawing and writing about 'myself'.
Week Two
Continue the same activity as in Week One.

Arts and Crafts Centre
Week One
Have children work in pairs. Have one child lie on a large sheet of paper on the floor while the other child draws around the one lying down. Then they take turns. An adult volunteer can help to cut around the body shapes. Then have each of the children dress and decorate their own body shape.

Week Two
Continue the same activity as in Week One.

Block Centre
Week One
Provide two number cards for each child. Have children build with the number of blocks indicated on their number cards. Encourage them to note similarities and differences between constructions.

Week Two
Have children work together while building one structure. Then take "Polaroid" pictures of the children with their structure. Display the pictures and use them to discuss cooperative behaviour.

Concepts/Skills Which May Be Developed

Reflecting on self
Early writing
Early reading
Self expression
Creative expression

Cooperation
Manipulation
Self awareness
Creative expression

Counting
Creative expression
Similarities
Differences
Comparing

Cooperation
Self expression
Sharing space

Sand Centre

Week One

Introduce scales and three different-sized sand dolls for the children to fill and to compare weights. Have children order the dolls from heaviest to lightest or lightest to heaviest.

Week Two

Introduce five cans with holes punched in the sides at different levels. Have children fill and order the cans from full to almost empty.

Home Centre

Week One

Introduce a full length mirror, and focus the children's attention on their similarities and differences.

Week Two

Introduce a variety of hats, wigs, and scarves for the children to wear. Then have them look at themselves in the mirror.

Concepts/Skills Which May Be Developed

Weighing
Comparing
Same/different
Ordering

Ordering
Pressure of sand
Levels of sand
Comparing

Likenesses
Differences
Comparing
Accepting self
Sharing

Likenesses
Differences
Comparing
Role playing

Culminating Activity

Make class booklets in which each child illustrates and writes or dictates his ideas on one page. These pages may be stapled together to make a book for everyone to share. These books may also be displayed in the library. Some book topics may be as follows:

Kindness is . . .
Love is . . .
Co-operation is . . .

The body silhouettes made at the Arts and Crafts Centre may be displayed at children's heights in the hallway or on bulletin boards.

Resource Materials
Books

Bottner, Barbara. *Messy.* New York: Delacorte Press, 1979.

Delton, Judy. *Two Good Friends.* New York: Crown Publishers, 1974.

Delton, Judy. *Two Is Company.* New York: Crown Publishers, 1976.

Goffstein, M. *Neighbors.* New York: Harper and Row, 1979.

Rachlin, S. L., Ditchburn, S. J., Bannon, B., and Sawicki, E. *First Steps To Mathematics.* Calgary, Alberta: Braun and Braun Educational Enterprises Ltd., 1984.

Watanabe, Shigeo. *How Do I Put It On?* Markham, Ontario: Penguin Books Canada Ltd., 1983.

This theme covers a two-week period.

Major Objectives

To develop an awareness of the sense of touch, taste, smell, sight and hearing.

To develop an awareness of how the 'senses' help us to learn about the world around us.

Related Objectives

To develop an awareness of each of the senses and to be able to consider one sense at a time.

To develop the ability to describe how each of the senses is affected by certain things.

Motivation

Introduce a 'senses' table in the classroom on which materials emphasizing each of the senses is displayed.

For example:	Touch	fabrics of different textures
	Sight	items of various colours, e.g., pegs and peg board
	Hear	boxes of objects which rattle, clank, swish, etc.
	Smell	sniffing bottles containing cloves, onion, chocolate, etc.
	Taste	foods of varying tastes such as sweet, sour, salty, spicy, etc.

Large Group Activities

Focus on a different 'sense' each day. Provide materials or activities related to each sense that will encourage ideas. Examples of materials and activities for each of the senses follows:

Touch — Provide fabric swatches of different textures, shells, bricks, glass, corrugated cardboard, stone, marshmallows, rubber, cork, etc.

Sight — Play the game 'I Spy' and focus on shapes and colours of objects in the room.

Hearing — Provide tapes of farm, school and home sounds. Also go for a walk to listen to and identify outdoor sounds.

Smell — Provide small containers of materials such as perfume, paint, cloves, cinnamon, lemon, shaving lotion, baby powder, etc.

Taste — Provide a variety of materials in cups such as chocolate, lemon juice, vanilla, honey, vinegar, mustard, etc. Provide each child with popsicle sticks to taste the materials.

Brainstorm and record words to describe a different 'sense' each day.

See Resource Materials for films that could be shown and books that could be read to the children.

Discussion Topics

- Discuss each of the senses and the body part or parts related to it.
- Present discussion cards, each containing a different question related to any one of the senses. A child may choose a card which can be read by the teacher and responded to by the child. Some examples follow:

How does butter feel?

How does sugar taste?

What does a car sound like?

What does snow look like?

What does toothpaste smell like?

- Present 'feely' bags containing different objects such as sponges, stones, clothespins, toy cars, etc. Encourage the children to take turns describing the object they feel while the rest of the class guess what it could be.
- Discuss foods (e.g., potatoes, meat, etc.) that change in smell or taste during cooking. This may also be demonstrated.
- Blindfold children and have adults or older children take them for a walk. Then discuss how it would feel to be blind.

Centre Activities

Home Centre
Week One
Introduce baby soap, baby powder, and empty perfume and shaving lotion bottles.

Sensory awareness
Role playing

Week Two
Change the Home Centre into an Optometrist office. Introduce a white coat for the Optometrist, eye glass frames without lenses, and two eye charts, one with large lower case letters and the other with numbers from one to ten.

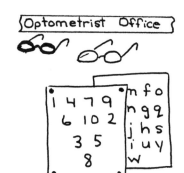

Role playing
Letter recognition
Number recognition

```
a   l   m   f   o
p  b  k  n  g  q
z  r  c  j  h  s
x  t  d  i  u  y
    v  e  w
```

```
   1   4   7   9
     6  10  2
       3   5
          8
```

Mathematics Centre
Week One
Provide a variety of smelly stickers for the children to classify on a graph according to whether they like them/do not like them.

Early graphing
Smells
Counting
Comparing
Classifying

I like						
I do not like						

Week Two
Introduce a sheet on which the outline of a variety of objects (e.g., paper clips, scotch tape, etc.) has been drawn. Provide the objects and the children may place them on the appropriate outline.

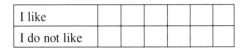

Shapes
Outline of shapes
Sense of touch
Relating shape to object

Introduce a 'feely' bag game. Objects are placed in the feely bag one at a time and the children must guess what they are by feeling them in the bag.

Outline of shapes
Sense of touch
Relating shape to object

Carpentry Centre
Week One
Introduce a variety of different kinds of soft woods like poplar or spruce. Encourage the children's awareness of the smell of each kind of wood. Provide paper for drawing plans, a tape measure, glue, hammer, and nails for the children to construct things out of the wood.

Sensory awareness
Planning
Measurement
Creative expression
Coordination and skill in use of tools
Relating plans to project

Week Two
Continue as in Week One.

Language Arts Centre

Week One

Provide paper bottle shapes and different samples of sensory materials such as textured fabric, cloves, fun fur, tin foil, chocolate, coffee grounds, etc. Have children glue the material onto the bottle shapes. They may also dictate and then copy stories about their sensory experiences onto another bottle-shaped paper.

Week Two

Introduce word cards and a variety of pictures at the wall pocket chart.

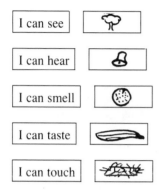

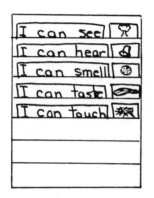

Have the children place the pictures in the appropriate sentences.

Concepts/Skills Which May be Developed

Sensory awareness
Creative expression
Vocabulary to describe the senses
Early reading
Early writing

Early reading
Language patterns

85

Cooking Centre

Week One

Provide popcorn, and popcorn makers. Have children make strings of popcorn to feed to the birds. Encourage the children to discuss the smell of popcorn and the appearance of the kernals before and after popping.

Week Two

Describe the powder form of Jello, the liquid form, and after it is set. Have the children taste the Jello in each of the stages.

Concepts/Skills Which May Be Developed

Smells
Tastes
Consideration for birds
Comparing
Vocabulary to describe the senses

Smells
Tastes
Change in form
Comparing
Vocabulary to describe the senses

Paint Centre

Week One

Introduce finger painting, using chocolate and vanilla pudding. Having children finger paint on paper with a shiny surface or on a table top. Encourage them to discuss the taste, smell, and feel of the pudding.

Week Two

Continue the same activity as in Week One.

Smells
Tastes
Feel of pudding
Creative expression

Arts and Crafts Centre

Week One

Mix tempera paint and pour into two pie plates. Have children make hand prints on large sheets of white paper. Encourage discussion of how the paint feels.

Week Two

Pour tempera paint into a pie plate. Spread large sheets of white paper on the floor for the children to walk across after they have stepped into the paint. Then have the children wash their feet in plastic pails of soapy water. Encourage discussion of how the paint feels and how the water feels.

Tactile sensations
Vocabulary
Creative expression
Self expression

Tactile sensations
Vocabulary
Creative expression
Self expression

Culminating Activity

Go for a walk in the community and take along a tape recorder and have children record which of the senses they are using. Back in the classroom have a tasting party and listen to the tape recordings made on the walking trip.

Resource Materials

Films

Health — Your Senses and Their Care, 11 minutes, Charles Cahill and Associates, 1968.
Learning With Your Senses, 11 minutes, Coronet, 1967.

Books

Aliki. *My Five Senses.* New York: Thomas Y. Crowell, 1962.
Bram, Elizabeth. *One Day I Closed My Eyes And The World Disappeared.* New York: Dial Press, 1978.
Brown, Marcia. *Touch Will Tell.* New York: Watts, 1979.
Charles, Donald. *Calico Cat's Rainbow.* Chicago: Children's Press, 1975.
Keats, Ezra Jack. *Goggles.* New York: Macmillan, 1969.
Le Sieg, Theo. *Eye Book.* New York: Random House, 1968.
Ward, Brian. *Touch, Taste, And Smell.* London: F. Watts, 1982.

This theme covers a one-week period.

Major Objectives

To develop an understanding of the special day called Valentine's Day.

To relate valentines to friendship and kindness.

Related Objectives

To develop an awareness of Valentine's Day symbols such as hearts, cupids, arrows, and lace.

To develop an interest in recognizing and writing the names of others.

Motivation

Introduce a mailing system made from milk cartons glued together. Give each child a list of manuscript written names of the children in the class. Have the children write the names of their friends on their valentines and use the mailing system to mail them.

Large Group Activities

Show the film *Winnie The Pooh and Tigger too*. Discuss how Rabbit, Pooh, and Piglet plan to change Tigger and then how they decide that Tigger should just be himself.

Introduce the following finger play:

Valentine's Day

Flowers are sweet, this is true.
But, for my valentine I'll choose you (each child points to another).

Brainstorm and record the children's ideas of what love is on sheets of paper. Encourage ideas such as 'love is when my mother hugs me' or 'love is when I help someone'. Copy the ideas onto cloud shapes and paste these onto a large blue sheet to make a mural. Title the mural "Love is . . ." and display it on the bulletin board.

See Resource Materials for a film that could be shown and books that could be read to the children.

Discussion topics

- Discuss Valentine's Day customs.
- Discuss the symbols for Valentine's Day such as hearts, cupids, arrows, and lace.
- Discuss plans for a Valentine's Day party. Consider food, drinks, decorations, games, and sharing valentines.

Centre Activities

Cooking Centre
Week One

Make sugar cookie dough (see Resource Materials for recipe and chart-sized pictures) with the children. Then have children roll out the dough, and cut out cookies using heart-shaped cookie cutters. When the cookies are baked and cooled, have children decorate them for the Valentine's party.

Concepts/Skills Which May be Developed

Early reading
Manipulation
Associating pictures and words
Measuring
Counting
Creative expression

Manipulation Centre
Week One

Provide red-coloured salt playdough (see the Theme "Apples" for the recipe), heart-shaped stencils, plastic knives, and rolling pins for the children to make heart necklaces. Make a large hole for the necklace string in each heart. Then bake the hearts at 100°C (200°F) for one hour. The hearts may be painted with tempera paint and dipped in shellac the following day. After they are dry, help the children string their hearts to make a necklace.

Language Arts Centre
Week One

Introduce the following poem in the wall pocket chart:

> If I could be a valentine

> I'd run down the street

> And say loving messages

> To every child I'd meet.

Make a set of individual word cards for the children to match to those on the strips.

Also, make substitute words with picture clues for the word 'valentine'. Some examples follow:

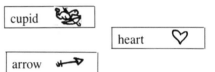

Writing Centre
Week One

Have children make their valentines from a selection of old valentine cards. Provide a variety of messages which they may copy onto their valentines. For example:

> Roses are red
> Violets are blue
> Sugar is sweet
> And so are you.

> I love you.

> You are my friend.

> I like you.

Home Centre
Week One

Provide pairs of large hearts cut from red material for each child. Have children sew two hearts together with overcast stitches and stuff them with foam chips to make cushions.

Arts and Crafts Centre
Week One

Provide tissue paper hearts of various sizes and colours. Have children make placemats for the party by gluing small hearts in patterns on a large heart.

Concepts/Skills Which May Be Developed

Manipulation
Shapes
Creative expression

Early reading
Early writing
Classification
Matching

Early reading
Early writing
Letter recognition
Manuscript writing

Manipulation
Role playing
Creative expression

Creative expression
Patterning
Space and Shapes
Planning

Sand Centre
Week One

Pour water onto the sand to make it wet. Introduce heart-shaped molds and scales. Have children make valentine-shaped cakes with the sand. These cakes may be compared for size and weight.

Concepts/Skills Which May Be Developed

Properties of wet sand
Molding sand
Role playing
Size comparisons
Weight comparisons

Culminating Activity

Plan a Valentine's party at which the placemats made at the Arts and Crafts Centre may be used. Serve red jello, the cookies that were baked and decorated at the Cooking Centre and red juice in styrofoam cups decorated with red hearts. Decorate the doorway with red and white crepe paper.

Resource Materials

Films

Winnie the Pooh and Tigger Too, 20 minutes, Walt Disney Productions, 1974.

Books

Barkin, Carol. *Are We Still Best Friends?* Chicago: Raintree Editions, 1975.
Burningham, John. *Friend.* London: Cap, 1975.
Delton, Judy. *Two Good Friends.* New York: Crown Publishing, 1974.
Delton, Judy. *Two Is Company.* New York: Crown Publishing, 1976.
Duvoisin, Roger. *Periwinkle.* New York: Knopf, 1976.
Goffstein, M. *Neighbors.* New York: Harper and Row, 1979.
Mariana. *Miss Flora McFlimsey's Valentine.* New York: Lothrop, Lee and Shepard, 1962.

Recipes

Sugar Cookies

125 mL shortening
250 mL sugar
1 well-beaten egg
25 mL milk
5 mL vanilla

Beat above ingredients until light and fluffy.

Blend or sift the following ingredients together:

500 mL flour
10 mL baking powder
1 mL salt

Add dry ingredients to liquid ingredients.
Roll dough out on a floured surface.
Cut out with cookie cutters.
Bake on greased cookie sheet at 190°C (375°F)
 for six minutes.

This theme covers a two-week period.

Major Objectives

To develop a positive attitude towards hospitals.

To develop an awareness of the kinds of things that happen in hospitals.

Related Objectives

To develop an awareness of the kinds of work people do in hospitals.

To develop an awareness of various tools and equipment used in hospitals, and to be able to describe how they are used.

Motivation

Arrange a class visit to a children's hospital or children's ward of a general hospital. Obtain pictures of hospitals and equipment or borrow a variety of tools and equipment to encourage discussions following the hospital visit.

Large Group Activities

Do the following finger plays, suiting actions to words:

The Flu

Cock-a-doodle-do
My dolly has the flu,
I put her right to bed
For that's the thing to do.

Cock-a-doodle-do
I guess I've got the flu,
I caught it from my dolly,
Ca-choo, ca-choo, ca-choo.

Doctor Day

My mother said, "It's doctor day"
Then she and I were on our way
To see our friend the doctor who,
Would check on me as doctors do.
He had more things than I can tell
To help him keep the people well.
He checked me up and all the while
He wore a big and friendly smile.
So now I hope that someday you
May go to see the doctor too.

Make two sets of sentence strips of the finger play "The Flu". Place one set in the wall pocket chart. Have the children put the other set of sentences in sequential order and then match them to the set in the wall pocket chart.

The Flu

Cock-a-doodle-do	Cock-a-doodle-do
My dolly has the flu,	I guess I've got the flu,
I put her right to bed	I caught it from my dolly,
For that's the thing to do.	Ca-choo, ca-choo, ca-choo.

Brainstorm and record 'hospital' vocabulary prior to going for a visit to the hospital. These words should be recorded in one colour and the vocabulary brainstormed following the visit should be recorded in another colour. See below for examples of words which may be brainstormed:

crutches	thermometer	patient	casts
medicine	stethoscope	hospital	doctors
nurses	beds	pills	wheelchairs
needle	visitors		

Record brainstormed words on word cards. Make duplicate cards of each word so that the words may be scrambled and matched on the floor, on the table, or in the pocket chart.

pills	pills	casts	casts	needles	needles	beds	beds

See Resource Materials for films that could be shown and books that could be read to the children.

Discussion Topics

- Discuss why people go to hospitals.
- Discuss what happens in a hospital.
- Discuss the jobs of different people in a hospital.

Centre Activities

Concepts/Skills Which May be Developed

Home Centre
Week One
Convert into a Hospital Centre by introducing white shirts, green gowns, gauze bandages, Teddy Bears, safety symbols on labels, pill bottles, a stethoscope, and empty syringes.
Week Two
Continue as in Week One.

Role playing
Vocabulary
Sharing and cooperation
Early reading

Mathematics Centre
Week One
Introduce cards with different numbers of band-aids glued on each. Have children count the number of band-aids on each card and place the appropriate number beside it.

Number recognition
Counting
One-to-one correspondence
Role playing

Week Two
Introduce empty pill bottles which have a different number up to ten written on each. Also provide paper and scissors and have the children cut out the appropriate number of 'pills' for each bottle.

Number recognition
Counting
One-to-one correspondence
Manipulation

Language Arts Centre
Week One
Introduce pairs of the following 'hospital' word cards:

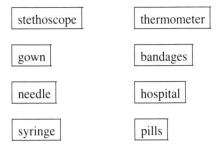

stethoscope	thermometer
gown	bandages
needle	hospital
syringe	pills

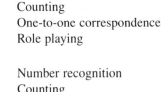

Early reading
Classification
Comparing

Place one set of word cards in the wall pocket chart. Have children match the other set to the words in the wall pocket chart.

Have children copy 'hospital' words into unlined pill bottle-shaped booklets.

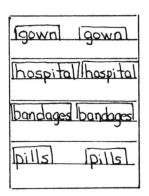

Early reading
Early writing
Manipulation
Handwriting

Week Two
Have a typewriter available for the children to type the 'hospital' words.

Introduce bottle shapes cut from construction paper (see Resource Materials for pattern) and white square labels. Have the children dictate and then copy their directions for the medicine in their 'bottles' on the labels.

Manipulation
Letter recognition and matching
Self expression
Early reading
Early writing

Block Centre
Week One
Provide wooden people, ambulances, houses and cars to encourage the children to build hospitals with blocks as they role play. Also provide blank word cards on which the children may copy 'hospital' words to be used as labels on their constructions.

Week Two
Continue with the same materials as in Week One.

Water Centre
Week One
Introduce plastic eyedroppers, medicine bottles, and coloured water. A black felt-marker line should be made at a different level on each medicine bottle. Have children fill bottles to the level indicated.

Week Two
Introduce clear plastic tubing, clear containers and coloured water. Demonstrate how the children may syphon the water from one container to another.

Carpentry Centre
Week One
Provide blank paper. Have children draw their plans for hospital constructions on the paper. Then introduce soft wood, a hammer, nails, and glue to be used in their constructions.

Week Two
As in Week One, have children draw plans on paper before constructing hospitals. Provide tempera paint for painting the constructions when completed. Then have children dictate and copy stories about their constructions onto blank paper.

Concepts/Skills Which May Be Developed

Role playing
Creative expression
Early reading
Early writing
Handwriting

Measurement
Comparing
Counting

Flow of water through tubing
Measurement
Syphoning

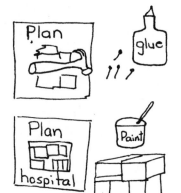

Planning
Creative expression
Vocabulary
Manipulation

Planning
Creative expression
Vocabulary
Manipulation

Culminating Activity

Arrange for a classroom visit by the school nurse. Have her discuss her job as a nurse and tell the children the kinds of things she does in the school setting.

Set up displays of materials used or produced at each centre and have three or four children in charge of each centre. Then invite the Year One children in to visit each centre in small groups and talk with the E.C.S. children about what they did at each centre. For example they labelled pill bottles at the Language Arts Centre and measured coloured water at the Water Centre.

Resource Materials
Films

If You Go To The Hospital, 15 minutes, 21 Inch Classroom, 1974.
Ripples Going To The Hospital, 15 minutes, National Instructional Television, 1970.
Ripples' Overnight In The Hospital, 15 minutes, National Instructional Television, 1970.

Books

Bruna, Dick. *Miffy In The Hospital.* New York: Methuen, 1978.
Rey, Margret and Rey, H. A. *Curious George Goes To The Hospital.* Boston: Houghton Mifflin Co., 1966.
Sachs, Elizabeth-Ann. *Just Like Always.* New York: Atheneum, 1981.

Pills ⚬⚬

Take ___ pills before lunch.

From:

Dr. ___

Pills ⚬⚬

Take ___ pills after breakfast.

From:

Dr. ___

Pills ⚬⚬

Take ___ pills before going to bed.

From:

Dr. ___

Pills ⚬⚬

Take ___ pills after dinner.

From:

Dr. ___

This theme covers a two-week period.

Major Objectives

To develop an awareness of reality and fantasy.

To develop an awareness of the many kinds of little people such as elves, trolls, fairies, gnomes, and leprechauns.

Related Objectives

To develop creative thinking about little people.

To develop vocabulary related to little people.

Motivation

Show the film *Elves And The Shoemaker* and discuss how the elves look, how they act, and what they do. Read a story such as Gillian Guile's *Snow White,* and discuss how the dwarfs look, how they act, and what they do. Then discuss similarities and differences between elves and dwarfs.

Large Group Activities

Do the following finger plays, suiting actions to words:

Elves

This little elf likes to hammer.
This little elf likes to saw.
This little elf likes to splash or paint.
This one has pictures to draw.
And this little elf likes best of all
To put the cry in the baby doll.

Suppose

Do you suppose a giant
Who is tall, tall, tall,
Could ever be a brownie
Who is small, small, small?
But the brownie who is tiny
Will try, try, try
To reach up to the giant
Who is high, high, high.

Creative movement activities may include moving like elves, gnomes, fairies, trolls, and leprechauns.

Brainstorm and record words that describe what each of the 'little people' eat, where they sleep, where they live, and what they like to do. Categorize the ideas onto separate sheets so that more ideas can be added as the theme progresses.

Introduce the story *Brown Bear, Brown Bear* (Martin, 1967) in the wall pocket chart. Use this story pattern to make new stories. For example:

Little	Elf	Little	Elf

Happy	Brownie	Happy	Brownie

See Resource Materials for films that could be shown and books that could be read to the children.

Discussion Topics

- Discuss similarities and differences between little people.
- Discuss why we like stories about little people.
- Discuss the fantasy and reality in stories about little people.
- Discuss ways in which we can be like little people.

Centre Activities

Block Centre
Week One
Provide little wooden people. Have children build homes for them using small coloured blocks.

Role playing
Planning
Manipulation
Creative expression

Week Two
Include a variety of building materials such as Lego, Mechanno, and Loc Blocs for the children to build homes for little people. Blank paper and coloured pencils should be available for the children to draw plans.

Creative expression
Role playing
Planning
Early writing

Paint Centre
Week One
Provide small-sized paper and small paint brushes for the children to paint little people.

Creative expression
Manipulation
Early writing

Week Two
Provide white art paper, crayons, and a thin black paint or wash. Have children draw and colour little people, a moon, and stars on their paper. Then have them paint over the pictures with the paint-wash. It will look like small people in the dark.

Creative expression
Manipulation
Early writing

Mathematics Centre
Week One
Introduce five sets of little people (e.g., elves, brownies and dwarfs) with a different number in each set. Provide a graphing format (see page 17 and 18 in Rachlin, et. al., 1984) so that the children may graph the number of each kind onto the format. Discuss the terms 'most', 'least', and the 'same'.

Counting
One-to-one correspondence
Graphing
Comparing

Week Two
Provide paper elf shoes and hats in various sizes and colours. Have children make patterns by alternating the colours and sizes of hats and shoes.

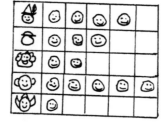

Colours
Sizes
Patterning

Arts and Crafts Centre
Week One
Provide junk material (e.g., boxes and scraps of fabric and paper). Have children make elves and elf homes. Provide unlined booklets shaped like elf shoes. The children may dictate stories to copy into their booklets.

Creative expression
Role playing
Textures
Early writing
Early reading

Week Two
Provide little paper people in a variety of shapes and sizes. Have children dress and decorate them with yarn and tissue paper. They may write or dictate a story about their little people.

Size and shape
Role playing
Creative expression
Early reading
Early writing

Writing Centre
Week One
Provide stamp pads, plain paper, and fine felt markers. Have children make thumb prints on the paper, then draw details on the print to form little people and little animals. They may also dictate and then copy stories about their people and animals.

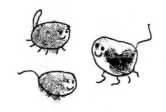

Week Two
Continue as in Week One.

Concepts/Skills Which May Be Developed
Shapes
Creative expression
Early reading
Early writing

Language Arts Centre
Week One
Review the story pattern from *Brown Bear, Brown Bear* (Martin, 1967) and the words for "Little Elf, Little Elf" introduced in the large group activities. Provide word cards and pictures for other small people, such as:

Early reading
Language patterns
Comparing
Matching

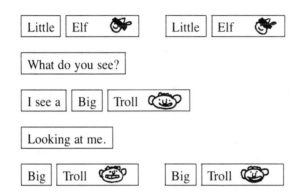

Follow the story pattern using the following:
Big Troll
Pretty Fairy
Tiny Troll
Green Leprechaun
Week Two
Continue as in Week One.

Culminating Activity
Show the film *Elves and the Shoemaker* with the volume turned off. Have the children tell the story in their own words while showing the film. Discuss and dictate ideas about things that happened in the film.

Resource Materials
Films
Elves And The Shoemaker, 30 minutes, Allan David Productions, 1967.
Books
DePaola, Thomas. *When Everyone Was Fast Asleep.* New York: Holiday House, 1976.

Guile, Gillian. *Snow White.* Don Mills, Ontario: General Publishing Co. Limited, (no date).

Martin, Bill. *Brown Bear, Brown Bear.* New York: Holt, Rinehart and Winston, 1970.

Rachlin, Sidney and Ditchburn, S., Bannon, B., Sawicki, E. *First Steps to Mathematics.* Calgary: Braun and Braun Educational Enterprises Ltd., 1984.

Zemach, Margot. *The Teeny Tiny Woman.* New York: Scholastic, 1965.

This theme covers a two-week period.

Major Objectives

To develop an understanding of the different roles of community helpers.

To develop an awareness of family members as community members.

Related Objectives

To develop the idea that each person's role differs in some way.

To develop the idea that people in society help one another.

Motivation

Invite parents or school staff to talk about their jobs to the children. Encourage the visitors to talk about what they do when they are not at their jobs. Are they parents? Do they live in a house? Do they have jobs to do in their homes?

Large Group Activities

Arrange visits from various community helpers.

Arrange visits to the Fire Department, Police Station, Hospital, Optometrist's Office, Super Market, Bakery, etc. Discuss the visit and write thank you letters as follow-up activities.

Make a group book about people at work. Have each child choose one person whose job they will write about, for example My Mom . . ., My Dad . . ., The School Secretary . . ., The Doctor . . ., etc.

Do the following finger plays, suiting actions to words:

I Am A Cobbler

I am a cobbler
And this is what I do:
Rap-a-tap-tap
To mend my shoe.

The Fire Bell

Clang! goes the fire bell
The trucks are coming fast,
Chief's car first
Ladder truck last.
Clang! goes the fire bell
Can't you hear it say:
"Here come the firemen,
Quick clear the way!"

See Resource Materials for films that could be shown and books that could be read to the children.

Discussion Topics

- Discuss the jobs of different adults in the school.
- Discuss what the children know about the jobs of their parents.
- Discuss what mothers do and what fathers do in their roles at home.
- Discuss the 'safety' roles of police and firemen, etc.
- Discuss the 'service' roles of garbage collectors, newspaper delivery people, barbers, etc.
- Discuss the 'health' roles of doctors, nurses, dentists, etc.
- Discuss the 'food' roles of bakers, farmers, grocers, etc.

Centre Activities

Home Centre
Week One
Introduce a variety of hats, purses and clothing for different occupations.

Role playing
Vocabulary related to job roles
Relating clothing to roles

Week Two
Continue activities from Week One. Provide empty lunch bags and pictures of food so children may pack lunches as they role play going to work. Place money in purses to encourage paying for things such as newspapers, bus trips, groceries, etc.

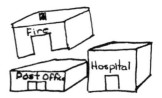

Role playing
Vocabulary related to job roles
Relating clothing to roles
Concepts about money values

Language Arts Centre
Week One
Provide empty boxes and scrap materials. Have children create buildings for various community helpers such as a fire station or hospital and label them. These buildings may be displayed on a bulletin board mural. The children may also write or dictate and then copy a story about their building.

Planning
Creative expression
Early reading
Early writing
Vocabulary related to community helpers

Week Two
Introduce a "Community Helper" bingo game in which each of the caller's cards has a labelled picture of a community helper (see Resource Materials for pictures). The player's cards should contain a variety of labelled pictures of community helpers. When the caller calls a name of a community helper, the players place a chip on the appropriate picture. Have children copy community helper words from the bingo game into unlined booklets.

Early reading
Cooperation
Early writing
Vocabulary related to community helpers

Arts and Crafts Centre
Week One
Provide large paper body shapes, glue and a variety of fabric scraps. Have children create the costume of a community helper on a paper body shape. Encourage the children to dictate a story about the helper they created.

Creative expression
Community helper awareness
Early reading
Early writing
Awareness of detail

Week Two
Introduce a large empty box and scrap materials for the children to work cooperatively while building a bus or fire engine with a speedometer, name of vehicle, etc. Encourage the children to dictate and then copy a story about their vehicle.

Creative expression
Awareness of detail
Early reading
Early writing

Mathematics Centre

Week One

Introduce a number bingo game in which each of the caller's cards has a number symbol and appropriate number of objects. The players' cards should contain a variety of number symbols and appropriate number of objects. When the caller calls a number the players place a chip on the appropriate number.

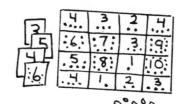

Number awareness
Cooperation
Early reading

Week Two

Introduce 100 cardboard milk carton shapes and twenty house shapes (see patterns in Resource Materials). The houses should be arranged along streets and each labelled with a number between one to ten. Have children wear milkman tags (see below) and place the appropriate number of milk cartons on each house.

Number recognition
Counting
Role playing
Early reading

Carpentry Centre

Week One

Introduce hard hats, vise, saw, screwdrivers, screws, and soft wood. Have children draw plans on paper for what they want to build before they begin building.

Planning
Gross and fine motor development
Early writing

Week Two

Continue as in Week One. Include blank booklets shaped like a hard hat, for children to illustrate and write about their constructions.

Planning
Gross and fine motor development
Early writing
Early reading

Sand Centre

Week One

Dampen the sand and provide several sizes and shapes of pans, bowls, and wooden spoons. Also provide baker hats and encourage the children to role play bakers in a bake shop.

Properties of wet sand
Vocabulary
Role playing

Week Two

Continue as in Week One. Include unlined booklets shaped like chef's hats for the children to illustrate and write about their bake shop.

Properties of wet sand
Vocabulary
Role playing
Early reading
Early writing

Block Centre

Week One

Introduce a variety of hats and display pictures of people involved in different jobs. Have children build with blocks as they role play.

Role playing
Planning
Creative expression
Early reading

Week Two

Provide toy cars, trucks, people, trains, houses and animals along with the blocks to encourage role playing.

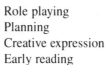

Role playing
Planning
Creative expression
Early reading

Culminating Activity

Take a walk around a nearby shopping centre. Discuss the different occupations held by people there, and how each of the businesses or offices helps people in the community.

Resource Materials

Films

Workers Who Come To Our House, 10 minutes, Coronet Instructional Media, 1974.
Everyone Helps In Our Community, 14 minutes, Churchill Films, 1963.

Books

Feder, Paula. *Where Does Teacher Live?* New York: Dutton, 1979.
Gergely, Tibor. *Busy Day Busy People*. New York: Random House, Inc., 1973.
Greene, Carla. *Doctors and Nurses*. New York: Harper and Row, 1963.
Greene, Carla. *I Want To Be A Dentist*. Chicago: Children's Press, 1960.
Lenski, Lois. *Policeman Small*. New York: Henry Z. Walck, Inc., 1962.
Merrill, Susan. *Washday*. New York: Seabury Press, 1978.

Patterns

Bingo

Mail Carrier

Chef

Nurse

Policeman

Doctor

Fireman

This theme covers a two-week period.

Major Objectives

To develop an awareness of spring as a season of the year.

To develop an awareness of the signs of spring.

Related Objectives

To develop an awareness of changes in the environment during spring.

To learn that spring usually brings windy days.

Motivation

Discuss the signs of spring that the children have noticed. Go for a walk around the school yard to observe the signs of spring. Talk about the wind, the water, the ice, the new grass, and the feeling of warmth in the air.

Large Group Activities

Do the following finger plays, suiting actions to words:

Falling Raindrops

Raindrops, raindrops!
Falling all around.
Patter-patter on the roof tops
Patter-patter on the ground.
Here is my umbrella,
It will keep me dry.
When I go walking in the rain
I hold it up so high.

An April Shower

Mix a little sunshine with an April shower,
Put in a flower bed and up pops a flower.

Provide long strips of coloured tissue paper or ribbon streamers. Have children move around the room, holding the streamers and making them fly high, fly low, twirl around, and flutter.

Have children take kites outside and move them by running fast, turning quickly, and by walking, etc.

See Resource Materials for films that could be shown and books that could be read to the children.

Brainstorm and record words that describe what kites can do, such as fly, flutter, dive, etc. Have the children copy the words onto small kite-shaped papers to make a bulletin board display or their completed sheets of paper can be stapled together to make a book.

Discussion Topics

- Discuss things that happen in the spring. For example, birds return, grass grows, tulips pop up, and other flowers begin to grow.
- Discuss the work of spring rain, the sun and the wind.
- Review safety rules related to playing on the street and playing with swings, skipping ropes, balls, and marbles while in the park.
- Discuss why people can fly kites best in the spring.
- Read, discuss, and review the sequence of ideas in *The Very Hungry Caterpillar* (Carle, 1970).
- Collect different kinds of kites, demonstrate, and discuss their similarities and differences.

Joys of Spring

Centre Activities

Concepts/Skills Which May be Developed

Home Centre

Week One

Provide a small screen-covered fan and hand windmills. Then encourage talk about the wind.

Wind as moving air
Role playing

Week Two

Provide the small screen-covered fan as in Week One. Introduce a clothesline, clothespins, a pan of water, and doll clothes. Have children wash and hang clothes on the line. Then turn on the fan. Encourage children to talk about the clothes drying and evaporation.

Wind as moving air
Role playing
Evaporation

Language Arts Centre

Week One

Make a 'clothesline' story using the story sequence from *The Very Hungry Caterpillar* (Carle, 1970). Cut out clothing shapes (see Resource Materials for patterns) from construction paper. Write words for foods listed in the story and glue appropriate picture clues on each shape. Provide a clothesline and clothespins so the children can hang these on the clothesline in the appropriate order.

Early reading
Sequencing
Story pattern
Manipulation

Week Two

Continue as in Week One, and have children copy the 'food' words into caterpillar-shaped booklets.

Early reading
Sequencing
Story patterns
Manipulation
Early writing

Block Centre

Week One

Introduce small wooden street safety signs, vehicles, pedestrians, and long strips of brown paper to be used for roads, together with a complete set of unit blocks. Have children build streets, etc.

Street safety
Early reading
Creative expression
Role playing
'Safety' vocabulary

Week Two

Provide the same materials as in Week One. Introduce unlined booklets which are titled 'Safety' for the children to illustrate and write about safety.

'Safety' vocabulary
Early writing
Self expression

Arts and Crafts Centre

Week One

Introduce Chinese fan making. Provide blank sheets of paper for the children to decorate on both sides with crayons, pencils, or felt markers. Fold the paper into narrow strips and staple together at one end. Spread out the other end.

Self expression
Creativity
Manipulation
Measurement

Week Two

Provide paper cups, scissors, and green scraps of construction paper. Have children cut strips down to the centre base of the cups, press the strips outward, and attach a stem and leaves made from the green construction paper. These flowers may be used to decorate the door and bulletin boards.

Small muscle development
Creativity
Measurement

Water Centre
Week One

Introduce sample pieces of various fabric such as silk, cotton, wool, corduroy, taffeta, etc. Also provide washboards, clothespins, and a clothesline. Have children wash the pieces of cloth and hang them up. Encourage the children to discuss how long each piece of fabric takes to dry.

Week Two

Continue as in Week One.

Mathematics Centre
Week One

Introduce geoboards, a variety of coloured elastics, and geoboard pattern cards for the children to copy.

Week Two

Provide blank geoboard cards and coloured pens, which match the colour of elastics, for children to draw their own geoboard pattern. Have children copy their own pattern by placing appropriate elastics on the geoboard.

Writing Centre
Week One

Cover a bulletin board with a large rainbow. Have children copy 'colour' words and 'spring' words and place them on the rainbow. Have them also cut coloured articles and 'spring' things from magazines and attach them to the rainbow.

Week Two

Provide rainbow-shaped unlined booklets for the children to copy words from the bulletin board display set up in Week One, and from other areas of the classroom, or from books.

Concepts/Skills Which May Be Developed

Evaporation
Different fabrics
Absorbancy
Manipulation

Space awareness
Shapes
Patterning
Measurement
Surface area

Space awareness
Shapes
Patterning
Measurement
Surface area
Planning

Manuscript writing
'Spring' vocabulary
Early reading
Early writing

Manuscript writing
'Spring' vocabulary
Early reading
Early writing

Culminating Activity

Provide paper, patterns, crayons, yarn, crepe paper, and instructions for everyone to make a kite. Read the instructions together before beginning to construct the kite.

Instructions For Making a Kite

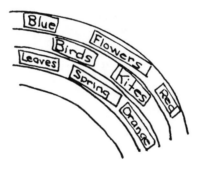

Choose a kite pattern

Trace the pattern onto a large sheet of paper

Cut the kite shape out of the large sheet of paper

Draw a face on your kite

Cut a piece of yarn as long as your arm

Staple the yarn to the bottom of your kite.

Decorate your kite

Fly your kite

Resource Materials

Films

Spring Is Here, 11 minutes, Four Seasons Series, I.F.B., 1967.
Kite Tale, 16 minutes, Murray Mintz, 1975.

Books

Beer, Kathleen. *What Happens In The Spring*. Washington: National Geographic Society, 1977.
Carle, Eric. *The Very Hungry Caterpillar*. Cleveland, Ohio: Collins World, 1969.
Domanska, Janina. *Spring Is*. New York: Greenwillow Books, 1976.
Hutchins, Pat. *Changes, Changes*. New York: Macmillan, 1971.
Tresselt, Alvin. *"Hi Mister Robin"!* New York: Lothrop, Lee and Shepard, 1950.

Patterns

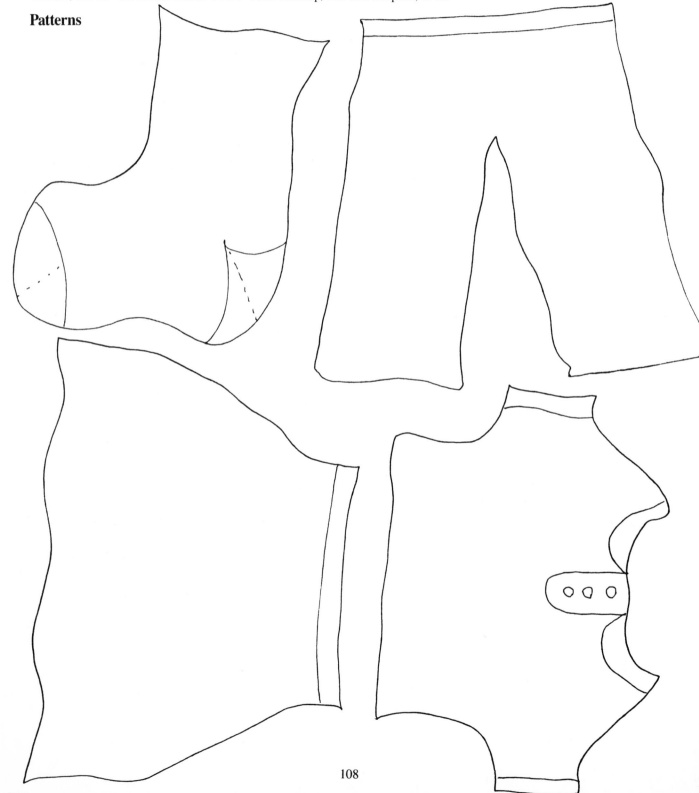

This theme covers a two-week period.

Major Objectives

To develop an understanding about farms.

To develop an awareness of the kinds of things that happen on the farm.

Related Objectives

To develop an understanding of the work people do on a farm.

To develop an awareness of the similarities and differences between farm animals.

Motivation

Show the film *Visit With Farmer Joe*. Discuss the animals shown in the film and how Farmer Joe takes care of them. Discuss plans for the class to visit a farm.

Large Group Activities

Introduce the following finger play in the wall pocket chart:

Two Mother Pigs

Two mother pigs lived in a pen (hold up thumbs).
Each had four babies and that made ten (show fingers and thumb).
These four babies were black as night (show four fingers).
These four babies were black and white (show other four fingers).
All eight babies loved to play,
And they rolled and rolled in the mud all day (roll hands over each other).
At night they curled up in a heap,
And squealed and squealed
Until they went to sleep (make fists, palms up).

Brainstorm and record ideas about work on the farm.

Brainstorm and record ideas about play on the farm.

Discuss and record things the children may see on the farm visit. Save the list so it may be added to during the brainstorming after visiting the farm.

Arrange a visit to a farm. Following the visit, add ideas in a different colour to those recorded before the visit. Count to see how many new ideas were added.

Discuss and record differences and similarities between living on a farm and living in a city.

See Resource Materials for a film that could be shown and books that could be read to the children.

Discussion Topics

- Discuss different baby animals, what they eat, how they look, etc.
- Discuss how to look after adult animals and baby animals.
- Discuss what animals eat and where they sleep.
- Discuss what each person in a farm family might do to help on the farm.

Centre Activities

Arts and Crafts Centre
Week One
Introduce weaving looms made by pounding nails into two ends of a wood frame. Provide sheep's wool, yarn, and natural materials such as hay and straw for the children to weave onto their looms.

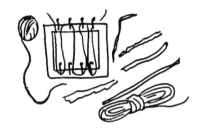

Weaving
Alternating threads
Properties of natural materials

Week Two
Continue weaving as in Week One, but include blank unlined loom-shaped booklets for the children to illustrate and write about their weavings.

Weaving
Alternating threads
Properties of natural materials
Early reading
Early writing

Paint Centre
Week One
Drop marbles into containers of tempera paint. Have children take one or two marbles out with a spoon and place them in a shoe box. As they rotate the shoe box the rolling marble will make painted lines in the box. Later the painted boxes can be decorated with natural materials from the farm such as grass, hay, straw, sticks, stones, etc.

Creative expression
Fine motor coordination
Properties of marbles
Properties of natural materials

Week Two
Continue activity as in Week One, but include unlined booklets for the children to illustrate and write about their paintings.

Creative expression
Early writing
Early reading

Language Arts Centre
Week One
Place the finger play "Two Mother Pigs" (introduced in the large group activity) in the wall pocket chart. Introduce duplicate word cards for the children to match to those on the chart.

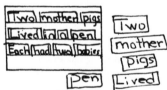

Early reading
Matching words

Week Two
Continue as in Week One, but have children dictate and copy stories about the farm into pig-shaped unlined booklets.

Early reading
Matching words
Early reading

Writing Centre
Week One
Have children match labelled pictures of mother and baby animals. Also provide barn-shaped unlined booklets for the children to illustrate and record names of animals.

Detail discrimination
Vocabulary
Early reading
Early writing
Manuscript writing

Week Two
Introduce unlined barn-shaped booklets with captions on each page. The title may be *My Visit To The Farm* and the page captions may be:

      I liked . . .
      I did not like . . .
      I would like to . . .
      My favorite animal was . . .
      My favorite farm job would be . . .

Early reading
Early writing
Manuscript writing
Recalling farm visits

Farm Centre
Week One
Display labelled farm pictures. Provide a variety of stuffed farm animals. Perhaps the children can bring some from home. Then they may dictate and copy stories about the farm into barn-shaped (see Resource Materials for pattern) unlined booklets.

Week Two
Farm Centre closed.

Sand Centre
Week One
Divide the sand in the sand table by placing a small board through the middle of the sand in the table. Leave half of the sand dry and add water to the sand in the other half. Provide toy farm animals, such as cows, ducks, pigs, and chickens. Have children place the animals in what they consider the most appropriate section. Then the children may dictate and copy stories about the animals into pig-shaped (see Resource Materials for pattern) unlined booklets.

Week Two
Continue as in Week One.

Mathematics Centre
Week One
Introduce dot-to-dot number sewing cards with farm picture outlines. Have children follow the numbers as they thread through the holes.

Week Two
Provide playdough and task cards which have space for the children to form things out of playdough and have suggestions for tasks such as:

- Make 6 chickens
- Make 5 pigs
- Make 1 farmer
- Make 3 cows
- Make a fence
- Make a pile of hay

Concepts/Skills Which May Be Developed

'Farm' vocabulary
Role playing
Early reading
Early writing

Properties of wet sand
Properties of dry sand
Role playing
'Farm' vocabulary
Early writing
Early reading

Sequencing
Counting
Fine motor coordination

Fine motor coordination
Early reading
Planning
Counting
One-to-one correspondence
Grouping

Culminating Activity

Arrange a follow-up visit to a farm to help the children clarify initial ideas and understandings. The visit may be followed by a discussion and review of some of the initial beliefs of the children.

Resource Materials
Films

Visit With Farmer Joe, 13 minutes, Walter Berlet and Myrna Berlet, 1975.

Books

Alexander, Martha. *Pigs Say Oink*. New York: Random House, Inc., 1978.
Bozzo, Maxine. *Toby In The Country, Toby In The City*. New York: Greenwillow Books, 1982.
Bruna, Dick. *Farmer John*. London: Methuen, 1984.
Hutchins, Pat. *Rosie's Walk*. New York: Macmillan, 1968.
Palazzo, Tony. *Animal Babies*. Garden City, N.Y.: Doubleday and Company, Inc., 1960.
Pomerantz, Charlotte. *The Piggy In The Puddle*. New York: Macmillan, 1974.

112

This theme covers a two-week period.

Major Objectives

To develop an appreciation for living things.

To develop an understanding of the similarities and differences between the needs of living things.

To develop an understanding of animate and inanimate things.

Related Objectives

To learn about the dependency of one living thing on another.

To develop an awareness of the characteristics of each living thing covered in this theme.

Motivation

Go for a walk in a park or in the school yard to look at insects, plants, and animals. Take along an insect collector which may be made by putting an empty can or plastic container, with both ends cut out, into a nylon stocking. The live insects may be put into the collector, observed in the container through the nylon, and then set free.

Large Group Activities

Brainstorm ideas for what there is about living things that lets us know they are living.

During creative movement, the children may move like living things or objects that are not living.

The children choose partners. One partner is a living thing (animate) and the other is an object (inanimate). The living partner will move the object around the room.

Do the following finger plays, suiting actions to words:

The Floppy Doll

Flop your arms,
Flop your feet,
Let your hands go free.
Be the raggiest rag doll
You ever did see.

Make a garden

Dig! Dig! Dig! Rake just so.
Plant the seeds, watch them grow.
Chop! Chop! Chop! Pull out weeds.
Warm rain and sun, my garden needs.
Up! Up! Up! Green stems climb.
Open wide, it's blossom time!

Two Puppies

Call the puppy,
And give him some milk.
Brush his coat
Till it shines like silk.
Call the dog
And give him a bone.
Take him for a walk,
Then put him in his home.

See Resource Materials for films that could be shown and books that could be read to the children.

Discussion Topics

- Name different animals and discuss their characteristics.
- Name different plants and discuss their characteristics.
- Discuss children and adults and their characteristics.
- Discuss animate and inanimate things.
- Discuss pet animals, zoo animals, and work animals.
- Discuss ways for taking care of plants, animals, people, and objects.

Centre Activities

Concepts/Skills Which May be Developed

Home Centre
Week One

Set up the Home Centre into a plant shop. Provide plastic plants, flowers, weeds and a variety of small real plants. Encourage the children to play store by providing price tags and play money.

Role playing
Vocabulary related to plants
Money (measurement)
Numbers
Early reading

Week Two

Introduce labels for items in the store, and 'Open' and 'Closed' signs (see Resource Materials for signs) for the store. Continue the plant store activity as in Week One.

Early reading
Role playing
Vocabulary related to plants
Money (measurement)
Numbers

Language Arts Centre
Week One

Introduce various pictures of plants, animals, people, and objects such as cars, houses, etc. Have children complete the following sentences in their desk pocket charts:

Early reading
Animate and inanimate characteristics
Classifying

 grows

 grows

 does not grow

 does not grow

Week Two

Divide the wall pocket chart in half with a strip of masking tape. Put the heading "Things That Grow" on one side and the heading "Things That Do Not Grow" on the other side. Have children classify the pictures from Week One into these two classifications.

Early reading
Animate and inanimate characteristics
Classifying
Graphing

Things That Grow	Things That Do Not Grow

Writing Centre
Week One

Provide unlined booklets titled "Things That Grow" or "Things That Do Not Grow." Have children illustrate and write in their booklets. They may copy some of the words from the pocket chart or go around the classroom copying words from charts and bulletin boards.

Early writing
Early reading
Self expression
Manuscript writing

Week Two

Continue activities as in Week One.

Sand Centre
Week One
Remove the sand and replace with potting soil. Provide empty flower pots, a watering can and seedlings which can be obtained from a plant nursery. Have children transplant the seedlings, and take care of them. Provide booklets shaped like flower pots for the children to illustrate and to write about their plants.
Week Two
Continue as in Week One.

Mathematics Centre
Week One
Provide toy animals and birds for the children to sort and classify, e.g., number of legs, size, colour, where they live and whether they eat plants or meat.

Week Two
Provide glue, paper stems and various sized paper leaves and paper flowers of various sizes and colours. Have children make border patterns on sheets of paper using the flowers, leaves, and stems.

Carpentry Centre
Week One
Provide short boards, nails, and hammers for the children to construct plant boxes. Have children sand and paint the boxes.
Week Two
Provide flowerpots, potting soil and cuttings from spider plants. Have children plant the cuttings in pots which may be placed in the plant boxes constructed in Week One and used as gifts.

Arts and Crafts Centre
Week One
Provide clear water in plastic pails and wide paint brushes for the children to 'paint' equipment in the playground area. Discuss the concept of evaporation with the children.
Week Two
Provide a large sheet of paper for each child which has been divided into three sections titled Birds, Animals, and Plants. Have children cut pictures of birds, animals, and plants from magazines, and categorize them.

Concepts/Skills Which May Be Developed

Planting and transplanting
Properties of potting soil
Care for plants
Plants are living things

Classification
Comparing
Noting details

Patterning
Ordering
Creative expression

Creative expression
Planning
Fine and gross motor coordination

Planning
Creative expression
Care for plants
Fine and gross motor coordination

Creative expression
Evaporation
Fine and gross motor coordination

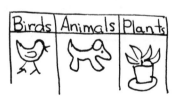

Classification
Comparing
Early reading

Culminating Activity

Take a walk in the community to point out and discuss things that are animate or inanimate.

A class project on "Things That Grow" and "Things That Do Not Grow" may be completed by having each child use one sheet of paper to illustrate and write about things that grow or things that do not grow. Then staple the sheets together to make a book.

Resource Materials
Films
What Do Plants Do? — A First Film, 11 minutes, Norman Bean, 1971.
Pigs, 11 minutes, Dimension Films, 1967.

Books
Burton, Marilee. *Elephant's Nest, Four Wordless Stories*. New York: Harper and Row, 1979.
Flack, Marjorie. *Restless Robin*. Boston: Houghton Mifflin, 1937.
Gackenbach, Dick. *Little Bug*. New York: Houghton Mifflin/Clarion Books, 1981.
Lobel, Arnold. *Grasshopper On The Road*. New York: Harper and Row, 1978.
Wildsmith, Brian. *Birds*. London: Oxford University Press, 1967.